PATRICK TREVOR-ROPER

THE WORLD
THROUGH
BLUNTED SIGHT

*An inquiry into the influence of defective vision
on art and character*

A NEW AND UPDATED EDITION OF THE CLASSIC WORK

SOUVENIR PRESS

First published 1970 by Thames & Hudson Ltd., London
Revised edition published 1988 by Viking
Published in paperback 1990 by Penguin
This edition, with additional material, published 1997
by Souvenir Press Ltd.,
43 Great Russell Street, London WCIB 3PA

ISBN 0 285 63397 X

10058478484

Acknowledgements are due to the editors of *The Proceedings of the Royal Society of Medicine* and *Annals of Ophthalmology* in which extracts from this book have appeared in a different form.

Printed in Great Britain by
Butler & Tanner Ltd., Frome and London

THE WORLD THROUGH BLUNTED SIGHT

For Herman Pasma.

CONTENTS

═══

LIST OF
ILLUSTRATIONS

Colour Plates

PREFACE TO THE FIRST EDITION

═══

Throughout these pages I have sought to trace the influence of altered vision on the personality of man; and, by reflecting on some writers and painters whose sight was impaired, to harness the nature of this impediment to the pattern of their artistry.

It is always rash for a scientist to venture from the solid shores of his exact science into such speculative waters; and, if I have seemed to flounder among too many unrelated disciplines, let me plead that, by constantly retreating behind the theories and experiments of others, I have tried to let these speak for themselves, and only rarely presumed myself to arbitrate. I am conscious, too, that I may have digressed more than a little on the way. Perhaps this also may be excused, for the marches of our subject are ill-defined, and there are some tantalizing pastures just off-course, into which it was a constant temptation to stray.

P T - R

PREFACE TO THE SECOND, REVISED EDITION

Eighteen years have passed since the first edition of *The World Through Blunted Sight* was published by Thames and Hudson. A further impression followed a few months later, and by the time this was exhausted more solid aspects of ophthalmology had usurped most of my time and energy. However, as the years passed, new evidences and new conjectures kept drifting in and, along with other appealing tit-bits of information, gravitating into that neglected file. So that once my days of hospital clinics had ended, the temptation to reappraise the whole issue became hard to resist, particularly since this offered me a chance to amend some slips and inadequacies which had gradually come to light in the original version.

The form of the first edition is retained, but some chapters have been substantially re-cast; many of the less relevant pictures have been replaced, and it has generally been possible to site our present illustrations at their appropriate points within the text, so as to ease the flow of reading. I hope that this new version will provide some refreshing thoughts on our wayward and ill-charted subject.

P.T-R.
1988

NOTE TO 1997 EDITION

With the republication of this edition, the opportunity has been taken to include a few small additional notes at various places in the text.

P.T-R.

INTRODUCTION

MAN IS A VISUAL ANIMAL. About half of the fibres that convey sensation to our brains stem from the optic nerves. We live in a world almost wholly orientated by sight, and we seek our food, sex and shelter through information provided by our retinal images.

The sense of smell, which dominated the lives of most of our vertebrate ancestors, has so shrunk in importance that it barely contributes to our sex and survival, and yields little beyond a minor aesthetic pleasure, principally when we are eating – and even then it generally fails to tell us if the food we are eating is poisonous, only warning us when it is indigestible through decay. The sense of hearing has never rated very highly in our evolutionary ascent. It emerged in our aquatic forebears as a refinement of the organ of balance; this told them whether they were the right way up, and whether moving, but had again shrunk in importance by the time man emerged, as our eyes largely usurped its function. Initially hearing helped our vertebrate ancestors to find mates; later it also became a way of signalling alarm and occasionally of asserting territory. But it has remained throughout evolution as a means of communication, and now has little relevance in helping us to assess the external world, except indirectly when we may need to fall back on the accounts of a better-sighted companion.

Just as the evolution of Stone-Age man entailed a gradual dominance of vision over the other senses, our subsequent history has witnessed a far greater change of evolutionary direction, almost as dramatic as the emergence of organic life itself; since, in this final phase, we learnt how to accumulate, outside the individual, the knowledge that each new generation acquired, so forming an ever-increasing repository for his successors to inherit. This latest super-evolution of man was made possible largely by his discovery of the art of abstracting ideas and images, which could then be projected orally or visually, and crystallized as pictures or, in schematic form, as a written language.

But in our new symbol-dominated lands that lie well to the East of Eden, it is not just the wisdom of the world that accumulates: each man-made imprint left for posterity carries with it also a reflection of the personality of its maker. And it is from a study of some of these imprints in our literature and art that we can sometimes look beyond the information they were intended to convey; in telling us something of the individual imprinter, they may also suggest an altered or impeded perception of the world he was representing.

For beneath our visual selves, beneath even the old Adam, lies buried that mammalian and pre-mammalian self, which feels and smells and intuitively or instinctively apprehends. When the dominating eyes are blunted, these 'older' senses again become the masters, and to that extent a new persona is born.

This, then, is the burden of the chapters that follow. The sight can be blunted in many ways; the retinal image can be distorted or blurred at certain distances, our colour values can be or go awry, our eyes can fail to work in unison, or the fields of our vision can shrink and finally the sight can be lost entirely.

The changes in personality that follow such a dulling of our sight are subtle and complex; and any psychological assessment of them would be suspect, because it would depend so much upon the attitude and experience of the observer. But in the outward expression of the personality, as crystallized in its writing and painting, we at least have a projection that admits an objective analysis, which applies not only to the personalities within our reach, but extends back in history to the days when artistry first emerged and the first ballads were sung.

It must be emphasized that the influence of any such physical and physiological factors on the pattern of our arts is, if present at all, almost inevitably of minor importance, and could rarely apply outside naturalistic paintings or writing. But in the final analysis, even these smallest factors should not be overlooked.

CHAPTER ONE

THE UNFOCUSED IMAGE

THE GREAT MAJORITY OF THOSE whose sight is poor have had their vision 'blunted' because of some optical imperfection in their eyeballs, so that they cannot receive a clearly focused image on their retinas, although the eyes are otherwise perfectly sound. Such optical anomalies can usually be neutralized by spectacles; but until the present century these were a luxury, normally chosen by trial and error from an itinerant vendor's tray, and frowned on by most nineteenth-century oculists, who held them to be damaging to the eyes.

But even if spectacles are worn, it is never quite the same as having a normal eye. Often the child has already suffered from his inadequacy before the glasses are prescribed, and he may well feel still more of an outsider when forced to wear these clumsy and fragile 'crutches'. Throughout life he knows he is different. And even those who escape the need for spectacles till the usual reading difficulties of middle age, face a potential psychological trauma with this first stigma of their gradual bodily decay.

To understand the optical basis of vision, we may consider the eyeball simply as a box-camera, spherical rather than cubical in shape, so that it can rotate easily within the orbit, but with almost identical components. Thus our adjustable pupil corresponds to the variable aperture of the camera's 'iris diaphragm', our cornea and lens (whose convexity can be augmented by contraction of the focusing muscle) correspond to the camera's convex lens (whose power can similarly be augmented for close range) and our retina corresponds to the film, both of these being placed at a fixed distance behind the lens, according to the focal length of the lens system.

But biology abhors the exact dimensions that are so integral in physics; and, just as the limbs and other bodily components vary in length and contour from the standard mean, so the eyeball is usually just a little longer or shorter than the ideal length that would permit an exact focus, or else the vertical and horizontal curvatures do not exactly match.

Those eyeballs that are slightly *shorter* than the optical ideal can compensate for this shortcoming by utilizing some of their internal focusing power (normally reserved for near-vision) in order to bring the focal point forwards, and so allow a clear image on the retina, which in this case lies closer to the lens of the eye; but this leaves less reserve of focusing power for seeing nearer objects; such eyes are thus 'long-sighted' or 'hypermetropic', and may need a supplementary convex lens in the form of spectacles to sharpen near vision.

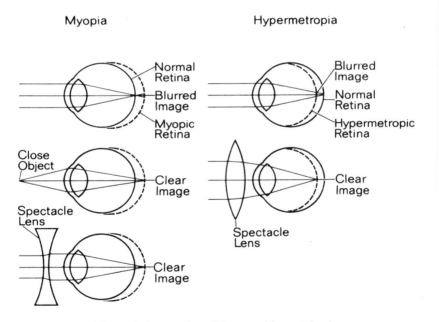

The optical correction of short- and long-sightedness.
In the myopic eye, only near objects are clearly focused, unless a concave lens is worn; in a hypermetropic eye, even distant objects may be out of focus, unless a convex lens is worn.

Old-fashioned cameras used to solve the problem of near-range not by adding a convex lens, but by being 'pulled-out', so that the lens system is made more distant from the film, as the nearer the object is to the camera, the further back from the lens its focal point lies. So when the eyeball is *longer* than the ideal, it finds itself, like the pulled-out camera, in clear focus for near objects only, whereas the distance is always blurred, unless compensated by wearing concave spectacles; and such long eyeballs are thus called 'short-sighted' or 'near-sighted' or 'myopic'.

The myopic (short-sighted) view: *near objects are in focus, but more distant objects become increasingly indistinct.*

The hypermetropic (long-sighted) view: *distant objects are in focus but nearer objects become increasingly indistinct.*

Short-sightedness ('myopia') and long-sightedness ('hypermetropia') are not specific failings of man; the shape of the eyes, as with other parts of the body, varies in every species; but a poorly focused retinal image is generally of little consequence in animals, who lack our sharpness of vision and whose world is primarily apprehended by smell, touch and hearing. However, it is of passing interest that while cats and dogs are usually normal-sighted and rats and mice, as the majority of wild animals, are long-sighted, myopia occurs quite commonly in horses and cattle (about 30 per cent), and also in monkeys, where the myopia may be extreme. Some myopic mammals have indeed been happily fitted with spectacles,[1] including award-winning retrievers and racehorses.* It has been suggested that those horses who readily shy at objects are just undiagnosed myopes.

*The spectacle firm of Dolland sought (in vain) to compete with their rival Aitchison by advertising 'horse goggles to promote high stepping'. Three years earlier the *Banner* of 13 January 1888 recorded that a horse, suspected of myopia and found by an oculist to have a 'number 7 eye', betrayed 'sedate enjoyment' of the concave lenses fitted, and 'whinnied in a plaintive minor key' when liberated from the stable without them.

A short-sighted racehorse being fitted for spectacles.

Among humans the proportions of myopes and hypermetropes are surprisingly constant in nearly all the Western races, 15–20 per cent being myopic and about 50 per cent hypermetropic; but in China and Japan myopia is about four times as common (60–70 per cent). Semitic races are also prone to myopia, often of high degree, while this is very rarely found among Nubians. The prevalence of high myopia in Egyptians and Jews as opposed to other Caucasians, in Europeans as opposed to Eskimos and African Negroes, and in Brahmins as opposed to non-Brahmins, has been attributed to their longer histories of civilization, the laws of natural selection (which would tend to weed out the less competitive high myopes in a primitive society) being relaxed in civilized groups.[2]

An elongated eyeball, however, is not just an isolated anatomical accident in any individual. No part of us is independent of the whole in its form or function; and the myopic eye, initially but one facet of an inherited mould of the human frame, may, in a limited way, continue to influence the development of that frame, its posture and its movements, throughout life. More especially is the myopic eyeball a part of a personality structure, with an influence on its evolution which may be of paramount importance.

The Myopic Personality

A sixth of the population are myopic, yet the normal-sighted tend to pay scant attention to this minor physical anomaly, and even the myope has usually come to terms with his built-in impediment, with only occasional calls to remind his fellows that it is more than just a tiresome blemish. As one eye-surgeon exclaimed recently to his assembled colleagues: 'But you don't understand, we myopes are different people.'* The myopes are an important, if unvocal, minority, with a common burden which, like every other impediment, may be either stimulating or damaging to the evolution of their characters.

That myopia and hypermetropia have some influence on personality is widely accepted – the studious and rather withdrawn myope and the extroverted hypermetrope are familiar figures; but as such generalizations, particularly about psychophysical groupings, are always suspect, we must approach with caution any more exact delineation of the personality patterns. Such an influence is inevitably greater when the ocular defect starts in childhood, and it is often tempered, but never annulled, by early recourse to corrective spectacles.

Concerning the typical myope, it would be difficult to better Dr Rice's rounded picture:[3]

A near-sighted child cannot do well on the playground because he cannot see. He will not like to hunt because he cannot see the game or the sights

*F.T.S. records one of his myopic patients whose difficulties in personal relationships yielded only after the prescription of contact-lenses (a common enough story); she explained that it took about three months after seeing clearly with her lenses before she could see clearly psychologically, and only at that point did her work start to improve.

of his gun. He will not like to tramp because distant objects are poorly seen and, for that reason, not appreciated. He will not like races or aviation or travel or sports of any sort. As a rule these persons do not like the theatre, or the motion picture, and are likely to have the idea that the latter, especially, is entertainment for children only, or, as they might say, for morons. It is because they cannot see the pictures clearly. But in school the situation is different, it is so easy to see and so wonderful to read as there are none of the diverting influences that draw the attention of the normal child, or the 'motor-minded' boy, to the fields, the parks and the woods. The child who knows that he cannot excel over his fellows in games gets a big satisfaction out of the conquest of the mind that he can command. After all, he reasons, this is what is really important. Ball games, hunting and fishing are a waste of time. What does it matter if one cannot do those things? He sees the fine details. When his classmates make mistakes the book-worm jumps to his feet with his hand in the air. He pleases his teacher but he loses his friends. He gets the reputation of being a know-it-all and a grind, and is popular only the days before the final examination. He does not count in athletics or parties, he is not 'one-of-the-bunch'. Such a child as we have described is not dependent on others for entertainment and is liable to grow rather contemptuous of the abilities of others. He does not adapt himself to the surroundings and is not willing to make compromises. He is often severe in his righteousness and his rightness and may become a disagreeable personage.

In contrast, here is Dr Rice's description of the typical hyper-metrope:[4]

Let us consider the farsighted boy, for example. His teachers have said of him that he is lazy, a mischief-maker, dumb, inattentive, or more sympathetic teachers have said that he is 'motor-minded'. His parents insist that he is bright enough but just won't study. He plays truant; he wants to quit school and go to work; he is more interested in girls and in athletics; he is out for a good time and is nearly always a jolly good fellow. If the child is a girl she is of the tomboy type. The 'motor-minded' boy does not correct his classmates when they make a slight mistake and so they like him. He cares nothing for fine details; indeed he does not know that they exist. The game's the thing! If the umpire did not see that he cut second base then it is just too bad for the other side. He will not stand out alone and stick for a minor point of principle. He is one of the boys; hail fellow, well met, and a jolly good fellow, and why not, he is happy and comfortable, at least when he is not required to do close-work indoors. He gets out in the fresh air and sunlight, he has a ravenous appetite because of his activity, he scarcely knows fatigue, except eye fatigue, which he avoids. He is tanned, masculine, very aggressive and is likely to be a devil with the women.

There have been several attempts to assess more exactly the personality changes that accompany myopia. Studies to correlate IQ rating and refractive error suggest that the myope is at any rate superior in pencil-and-paper types of intelligence – probably because of his greater reading ability and, among really gifted mathematicians, myopes are four times as common.[5] A recent report, from a follow-up of over 5,000 children, concluded that while the short-sighted achieve greater academic success, there is no evidence that they are more intelligent than their fellows. They did better at school even before their myopia developed – which might be attributed to a home tradition of bookwork, since their parents were probably myopic too.[6] They were more punctual, attentive at school, had more academic hobbies and less interest in sport than their normal-sighted fellows. This is perhaps not surprising, since some compensatingly useful gene would doubtless be needed for the survival of myopes in a primitive society.

There have indeed been many further analyses of the myopic personality (see Appendix 1), and other observations, less fully documented, that carry conviction, as upon the sleeping-habits of myopes, who tend to stay up late, for darkness is a great equalizer, and myopic children often feel more secure at night-time than their normal-sighted fellows. Mystics and religious leaders, as well as musicians and artists, are said to be frequently myopic, since a blurred view of the outer world is no impediment to their inner vision: perhaps these will all become fewer, as commercial enterprise and government subsidies commit a greater part of the population to wearing the spectacles which, in homogenizing the sight, may also shackle the spirit.

For what it is worth, we know from their preserved spectacles that the hypermetropes included Hindenburg ($+4.5D$)* and Martin Luther ($+3.0D$), while Bismarck ($-3.0D$), Schopenhauer

---

*The 'power' of spectacle lenses is measured in dioptres ('D'), negative ('−') when concave (as called for in myopia), and positive ('+') when convex (as called for in hypermetropia or presbyopia); about 3 per cent of the population have a high degree of myopia (rarely over -20 D) but the large majority of all spectacle lenses dispensed are beneath 5 dioptres in strength.

(-3.5D), Goethe (-6.0D), Schiller (-2.75D) and Marie An-
toinette[7] (-4.0D) were all myopic, as (it seems) were George
Washington, Louis XVI, Napoleon I,[8] Mary II,[9]★ Frederick II
('Stupor Mundi')[10]★ and (said Suetonius) Nero.

It is improbable that such a genetically determined anatomical
variation could be influenced by personality, rather than vice
versa; even so, some psychologists have suggested that, since the
basic personality pattern is normally fixed in early childhood,
well before the myopia has become evident, the primary change
lies in the personality; and a recent theory from Japan[11] seeks
to explain just how myopia can be induced by emotional
disturbances from an upset of the balance between cerebrum and
hypothalamus. Such echoes of the vitalism of our ancestors keep
turning up, but it seems amply established that nothing we can
do – no exercises or spectacles, diet or drugs – will have any
influence on the ultimate degree of near-sightedness, any more
than, by taking thought, we can influence the stature that our
genes have decreed.

That myopia is hereditary can indeed be illustrated where it
has left its mark down the family-trees of many distinguished
houses, with the characteristic personality and physical changes
that follow in its wake; however we face the inevitable difficulty
of all such historical diagnoses, for few surviving records have
any bearing on a condition that was, until the present century,
largely unrecognized and uncorrected.

Perhaps the best myopic pedigree available is that of the Medici
family compiled by Dr Alaerts.[12] As he tells us:

The doctor knows that every patient, especially the chronically sick, ends
by creating a new personality. The myope does not escape the rule; he has
an interior life different from others, a general bearing or a special personality capable of placing him in the limelight if he is gifted or energetic,
or leaving him in obscurity if he is timid. With the Medicis we also find
ourselves in the presence of a special mentality, a complex of infirmities,
but not of inferiority, because we are dealing with gifted and especially
intelligent beings. It is probably that which had the unexpected effects on

---

★Mary II's eyes 'were greyish and pale and so short-sighted that to read she must hold the book
very close to her face'.

The Arab historian, El Aini,[10] says that Arabs who saw Frederick II in the East reported that,
what with his red face and feeble sight, you would not give more than a few pence for him in a
slave-market.

The earliest depicted concave glasses for myopia.
Painting by Jan van Eyck, 1436.★

their way of life, and which exerted its influence in creating the Medicean
epoch.

★ The earliest myopic glasses on record were painted by Jan van Eyck,[13] and one of the earliest
surviving pairs of concave spectacles (of -6.5D) is that presented by King Gustavus Adolphus to
the city of Augsburg in 1632, although it seems very unlikely that he ever wore them himself.
There is a record of 'negative spectacles' being purchased in 1492–5.[14] Convex glasses, to assist
reading, were recorded by Pliny, and may even date back to a suitably curved rock crystal
found at Nineveh, but the earliest depicted are in the S. Nicolo chapter house in Treviso (see
p. 26).

The Medicis also had a family history of gout (rheumatism?), which limited their physical activities but gave rein to their intellects; when, on top of this, they inherited good taste and

The earliest depicted convex glasses for reading.
From a wall painting by Tommaso da Modena, 1352.

intelligence, all that they needed was position and fortune to ensure their success.

Since their disabilities (gout and myopia), with few exceptions, precluded successful soldiering, their enterprise found its outlet in banking and, when they were financially secure, in scholarship and encouragement of the arts, reaching its zenith with Pope Leo X – able, artistic, corpulent, sedentary and myopic. He at least bears the only certain evidence of myopia, because of the concave

Pope Leo X *holding his concave lens.*
Painting by Raphael.

spectacle-lens he was using when Raphael depicted him. The evidence of myopia in the other Medicis rests primarily on the mention of bad sight, especially when they are recorded as reading well into an advanced age (none but Leo X is known to have used glasses), and secondarily on the less convincing records of the appearance of their eyes; for again and again we find mention of their 'beautiful large eyes'. The myopic eyeball is almost by definition a large eyeball, and for that reason also tends to be prominent, and usually has a large pupil; large eyes tend to be appealing, and the large pupil (as of children) may suggest the added freshness of youth.

Thus we read that the founder, Giovanni de Bicci (1360–1428), led a 'retired life', burdened by rheumatic pains, 'reading greatly in order to instruct himself up to an advanced age', and also that he had 'remarkable eyes'.

His son, Cosimo ('Pater Patriae', 1389–1464), also rheumatic, was a considerable scholar. 'In spite of an advanced age, he used to read calligraphic texts'; and his wife noted that he 'had the habit of half-closing the eyes', which he explained as 'necessary in order to see more clearly'.★

Both the sons of Cosimo inherited his poor health; and Piero (1416–69), known as 'The Gouty', who survived Cosimo, led a scholarly and retired life. A man of great taste, it was he who summoned Botticelli to paint his family; he is stated to have had 'the eyes of his family' and 'to have read up to the end of his life [fifty-three years] without glasses'.

Lorenzo the Magnificent (1449–92) was only twenty when his father died. As Machiavelli said, 'he was the greatest protector of art and literature, more than any other prince had been'; other authorities have recorded that he had 'bad sight', and that 'his sight was weak'. Although fairly tall and a lover of physical exercise, he was 'obliged to take care for his health'. He too had 'prominent eyes', although specific evidence of poor distance-sight is lacking. His brother Giuliano, who was assassinated at the age of twenty-five, was said to have 'brilliant eyes', and it is interesting that his portrait by Botticelli and also that reconstituted from contemporary paintings by Bronzino show downcast and half-closed eyes.[15]

Piero, the son of Lorenzo (1471–1503), also had 'remarkably beautiful eyes', and both of his portraits (one by Botticelli) show large 'pale grey eyes with heavy eyelids'. Giovanni, the second son of Lorenzo (1476–1521), who became Pope Leo X, had notoriously poor sight, and in Raphael's painting he carries in his

---

★This outward sign is the cause of the derivation of the word 'myopia' (μύειν ὤφ); cf. the hypermetrope (or far-sighted) who does not half-close his eyes, but tends to furrow his brow when reading.

hand the concave lens which he is even said to have worn as a monocle while hunting. His actual lens of -12.0 D has been preserved in the Museo di Storia della Scienza in Florence. If

Lorenzo de' Medici, *of whom it was said that 'his eyes were prominent' and 'his sight was weak'. Painting of the Forentine school.*

confirmation were needed, Dr Alaerts quotes from a further source that Giovanni 'read the letters always close to his nose'.

It would be labouring the issue to follow the Medici family much further, particularly among its less distinguished members, about whom relatively little has been written; but indirect evidence of short-sightedness often turns up. Thus Piero's granddaughter, Catherine de' Medici, who married Henri II of France,

Giuliano de' Medici, *with the prominent, downcast and half-closed eyes common in myopia. Painting by Botticelli.*

is described (from her portrait by Bronzino) as having 'the eyes of her race, rather large'. Towards the close of her life she wrote letters copiously, and it is unlikely that she used reading-glasses. Even the cadet branch of the family apparently did not escape this myopic taint. Thus Cosimo I (1519–74) had 'large eyes with heavy lids', and 'his pupils are too dilated for a man of forty'; and so the story continues down the line. Even the debauched face of the last of the Medicis shows the soft, large eyes that had graced so many of his nobler ancestors.

The Prose and Poetry of the Myope

The psychology or psychopathology of the myope is indeed such a wide issue that we must be content with the foregoing rather crude generalizations, as so many other factors are involved, and myopia is so common. But in the artistic expression of the individual we at least have some objective imprint of his personality that allows a more exact analysis. For this reason the writings, and especially the paintings, of the myope deserve more detailed inspection.

Many creative writers have been myopic – a considerably higher proportion than in the population at large because of the directive effects of myopia on the personality. Most striking is the influence on visual imagery, for the myope (unless he wears glasses constantly) necessarily tends to avoid describing details that are outside his limited focal range. Thus the romantic poems of the contemporaries Keats and Shelley provide an easy contrast. Keats has been labelled short-sighted and, although there are occasional descriptions (as of the Ambleside waterfalls) that seem to confound this, it could be argued that his philosophical approach – of avoiding detailed description 'so that there should be more room for the imagination' – was a rationalization of his own physical defect. Certainly his subjects are usually auditory ('Ode to a Nightingale', sonnets 'On the Grasshopper and Cricket', 'On hearing the bagpipes', etc.), or fanciful (faeries and dream images); and when they are indeed visual, he tends to recall 'beaded bubbles winking at the brim', or 'Grecian urns' and so on, well within a limited focal range, in contrast to Shelley, who endlessly deploys his romantic imagery on distant prospects of sky and mountain. And although Keats and Shelley both use colour-images copiously (cf. p. 75), those of Keats are generally related to specific tangible objects, while Shelley's simply register the abstract hue.

Tennyson's extreme myopia is frequently recalled in the memoirs of his son Hallam,[16] who also noted that his hearing was extraordinarily keen, which he held to be a compensation for his short sight. 'He was so short-sighted that the moon, without a glass, seemed to him like a shield across the sky.' Although Tennyson evidently had occasional recourse to spectacles (which have been preserved), his poetic interests centred on objects that he could view at very close range, or the evocative quality of sounds, such as those that haunt the cadences of his 'In Memoriam',* and his epithets often have a tactile quality — like the 'wrinkled sea', which recalls the poems of the truly blind (p. 167).

> He clasps the crag with crooked hands;
> Close to the sun in lonely lands,
> Ringed with the azure world he stands.
>
> The wrinkled sea beneath him crawls;
> He watches from his mountain walls,
> And like a thunderbolt he falls.
>
> 'The Eagle'

Dr Johnson[17] was almost certainly short-sighted, for he could not otherwise have read in old age without spectacles, but perhaps mainly in one eye, since he never wore correcting spectacles (with which he was quite familiar), and his distance sight was good enough for him to give a vivid description of the fish-catching antics of the pelican; indeed, he loved the theatre, although he admitted to Garrick that there were other incentives to his theatrical visits ('I'll come no more behind your scenes, David, for the silk stockings and white bosoms of your actresses excite my amorous propensities'). He said of his left eye, 'the dog was never good for much'; this may have been more short-sighted, or scarred from the ulcers ('phlyctenular keratitis') he apparently suffered in infancy.

Milton,[18] another presumptive myope, very rarely mentions

---

*His relative, the authoress Tennyson Jesse, who had also inherited his myopic gene, once made this revealing comment to her oculist, when he provided her with correcting spectacles: 'Now I see as clearly as I always see in my dreams.'

Samuel Johnson, *a presumed myope.*
Portrait by Joshua Reynolds.

birds and, when he does, as often as not it is the nocturnal song
of the nightingale, while in his rare use of colour imagery, it is
usually 'tactile' in quality. He once declared that (like Aristotle)
he could see only three colours in a rainbow; this was also noted
by Goethe,[19] whose theory of colour vision was among the first
that contained truth, and who again was very myopic, yet refused
to wear his glasses in public, and always objected to others wearing
theirs.

It would be easy to add to this catalogue other myopic poets, W. B. Yeats, perhaps, or Alexander Pope, who wrote:

> Weak though I am of limb and short of sight
> Far from a lynx and not a giant quite,
> I'll do what Meed and Cheselden advise
> To keep these limbs and to preserve these eyes.

Dante Gabriel Rossetti, whose father was blind in later life, was said (by the psychologist, Adler)[20] to have compensated for his own optical inferiority in his writing and painting.

Edward Lear's paintings and drawings are also typical of the myope, with the details and clarity of a miniature, before he adopted a frankly pre-Raphaelite style. William Wordsworth's poor sight[21] was not, as sometimes suggested, due to myopia, but due to a lid infection by the trachoma 'virus' (which had reached England with the troops who were then returning from the Middle East war). He obtained some relief from the traditional treatment (a copper-sulphate stick), but had many periods in which he could not read or write, and his trouble was aggravated by an already very nervous disposition. His understandable fear of blindness is echoed in the words of the Wanderer in 'The Excursion' (IV.11.109):

> If the dear faculty of sight should fail
> Still it may be allowed me to remember
> What visionary powers of eye and soul
> In youth were mine.

Finally – James Joyce: 'As a 6-year-old pupil in a Jesuit school, the weakness of his eyes became manifest, and glasses, that shameful curse of the small lad, were forced upon him'; and he battled on, 'with weak eyes covered by spectacles, thin bony arms and legs, almost effeminate hands and feet, highly nervous and fearful' until, nineteen years later, he had the first of a series of attacks of iritis that were ultimately to whittle away his sight. These bouts of inflammation, affecting both eyes, and soon aggravated by a painful and damaging 'secondary glaucoma', dominated his life and thoughts. He underwent ten successive operations on his eyes, after which he could still just manage to read headlines, and an eleventh was threatened before he died from a perforated duodenal ulcer.[22]

Even before his sight was materially damaged he wrote this account of himself in the *Portrait of an Artist as a Young Man*:

Words. Was it their colours? He allowed them to glow and fade, hue after hue: sunrise gold, the russet and green of apple orchards, azure of waves, the grey-fringed fleece of clouds. No, it was not their colours: it was the poise and balance of the period itself. Did he then love the rhythmic rise and fall of words better than their associations of legend and colour? Or was it that, being as weak of sight as he was shy of mind, he drew less pleasure from the reflection of the glowing sensible world through the prism of a language many-coloured and richly storied than from the contemplation of an inner world of individual emotions mirrored perfectly in a lucid supple periodic prose?

As time went on, he increasingly withdrew into his interior world of associations and dream sequences, and his fascination with sounds became more compelling as his sight progressively worsened. Even in *Dubliners* he had written:

Every night as I gazed up at the window I said softly to myself the word paralysis. It had always sounded strangely in my ears, like the word gnomon in the Euclid and that word simony in the Catechism. But now it sounded to me like the name of some maleficent and sinful being.

As the associations of his words proliferated, they became enriched by his sheer pleasure in sound for its own sake, as in the frequent alliterations in *Ulysses*; and sounds, invented for their music as well as their associations, so permeated his last great work *Finnegans Wake* that the narrative only survives as a barely visible framework.

It must be remembered that all these inferences are simply loose conjectures, and it would be disastrous if any firm conclusions were drawn from such scattered examples of writers in whom this apparent ocular failing was one of the least components in their psychological pattern. We know that Edward Gibbon was significantly long-sighted,[23] for his convex spectacles ($+4.37$ D) have been preserved. Samuel Pepys was also long-sighted[24] (he probably also had a secondary 'latent squint') and found relief only when allowed in old age to use the glasses which had been denied to him earlier as being 'unsuitable for a young man'.

Among musicians myopia also appears to be common, perhaps with a similar association. Schubert (-3.75 D) and Wagner were frequently depicted wearing their myopic spectacles. Beethoven's[25] myopic lenses (− 4.0 D) have been preserved. J. S. Bach[26] was also moderately myopic, and it might be noted that he wrote one poem which has survived, a reflection on smoking his pipe − which was comfortably within his focal range. Gregor Mendel,[27] the father of genetics, would also have found his labours easily contained by his limited focal range; he later used myopic spectacles (− 4.5 D), and these too have been preserved.

The Art of the Myope

This simple physical deformity, of a rather long eyeball, which so affects the personality of the myope, his language and his orientation, may have an even more dramatic influence on his artistic style.

When a naturalistic painter is moderately myopic, he will probably see the canvas without difficulty, but not the more distant object he may seek to reproduce, and he is therefore reduced to painting what he sees, however blurred or distorted a percept it is. When he looks beyond the farthest point of his natural focus, detailed vision becomes increasingly unclear with relative clarity only in the essential lines and contours, resembling the 'peripheral vision', such as the normal-sighted person sees out of the corner of his eye.

The following personal account by L. Mills[28] describes graphically what the myope, and particularly the one with an added astigmatism, actually sees. The farthest point of his clear vision is only about 15 cm away; within this range, he says:

I appreciate fine and almost microscopic detail; but beyond this, and especially at distances over 6 metres, objects become greatly blurred and colours run together with curious blends and unusual, washed-out values. There is definite oblique distortion at far distances, differing in the two eyes, and often only the essential lines of form and contour provide the clues for identification of the object under examination. Such lines frequently take the jazzy mathematical shapes of cubism, and if I were a painter my conception often would be essentially geometric. At the symphony concerts my seat is in about the centre of the pit, nearly 70 feet from the stage. Three points of attention fix my interest at once: the tall form of the leader in the centre, attenuated like an El Greco drawing, two golden harps on the left flank and a strong white reflection from the curved, glistening, light-brown barrel of the bass drum, all striving for attention. The conductor holds the centre of interest, gyrating in strange contortions like some fearful wizard before a medley of misshapen geometric patterns in blacks, greys, whites and brown and gold; there are no details anywhere, merely blurred outlines of colour, form, light and movement ... The black clothes of the conductor and of the row of men next to the audience, that is, the men farthest from the strong overhead illumination, are jet-black, while the identical apparel of the rest of the musicians, directly under the lights, is grey-black, the contrast being sharp. When the harps are seen with one eye and then with the other eye, there is a prompt change in the angle of their inclination from the vertical, which represents the difference in slant given by the different degrees of astigmatism in the two eyes. The same change is noted in the size, shape and slant of the cellos and in the hands and faces. The vision of a single eye is much less distinct and brilliant than the combined vision, and distortion of objects is much more apparent with one eye than with the two eyes.

This 'peripheral' type of imagery is quite familiar to us, but usually taken for granted and rarely analysed, while for those who are short-sighted, it is the sort of view they always have without their glasses. It is also that employed by artists who aim primarily for effects of mass, line, colour and symbolism, just as it is often used by the lazy or the immature (as in primitive painting or child-art). This imagery was triumphantly exploited by most of the artists who came to be called Impressionists.

We can only guess whether Monet, who was the first to cultivate this peripheral type of vision, was myopic (conceivably as a sequel to his incipient cataract); but Cézanne is recorded as being myopic,[29] and one does not need to rely on the indirect evidence of his paintings. It is not surprising that only in some of his self-portraits are his colour values and optical proportions at all conventional. (Myopic spectacles were by then readily available; but, when this was proposed, Cézanne is said to have replied, 'Take those vulgar things away.') He incidentally suffered also from diabetes, so a little retinal damage may have further justified Huysmans' comment: 'An artist with a diseased retina, who, exasperated by a defective vision, discovered the basis of a new

Our peripheral vision
An attempt to illustrate the increasing loss of detail in the images we perceive from objects that lie further away from the point of our regard, as our peripheral retina registers only a relative clarity of the essential lines and contours.

art', or, as Ferry wrote (in *L'Eclair*, October 1906), 'An incomplete talent, in which an imperfect vision resulted in work that was always incomplete and sketchy'. So was Renoir, who, according to his biographer Vollard,[30] when looking at pictures would step back a few paces (in other words, out of his limited near-range of clear vision) in order to give it the effect of an Impressionistic picture. He was then sixty; and even at sixty-four, when none of us who are not myopic can expect to read at near range without convex spectacles, he liked to examine petit-point close to, taking it in his hands, and painted miniatures without them. He was said by his son to have once tried wearing glasses for reading, only 'to save his eyes', like Monet, who was said to have rejected the proffered spectacles, saying, 'Bon Dieu, je vois comme Bouguereau' (a conventional naturalistic painter of the period).[31, 20]

Degas too was myopic at least in one eye (Colour Plate I). He was able to paint landscapes in youth,[32] and his many self-portraits during early manhood show no glasses, but these may well have been executed within his limited focal range; his eyes were incidentally portrayed as rather prominent (see p. 28). He first described his loss of sight in 1871 (it was later attributed to his travails during the siege of Paris, although he had already been refused for the army because of poor sight). By 1873 Degas stated that his right eye was permanently damaged, and he became increasingly troubled by bright light which encouraged him to paint indoors, especially in a darkened studio, and to wear dark glasses. He also noted a blind spot in the centre of the field of his good eye, saying (to Sickert) that it was 'torment to draw, when he could only see around the spot at which he was looking, and never the spot itself'. So he almost certainly had damage to the macula (the central patch of retina) which could well be a degenerative change, either from a dystrophy (p. 135), a sequel to his myopia, or even to an 'iridochoroiditis' which was then diagnosed. The poor-sighted right eye may well have sustained a similar and more severe damage earlier. About 1893 some spectacles were ordered (now in the Musée d'Orsay) that covered the right eye and left only a small slit on the left lens; this was a device of Professor Landolt to relieve an irregular astigmatism, which might conceivably have followed corneal ulcers – possibly indeed provoked by exactions during the siege of Paris; but they evidently did not help much. As time passed he was often reduced to painting in pastel rather than oil as being an easier medium for his failing sight. Later, he discovered that by using photographs of the models or horses he sought to depict, he was able to bring these comfortably within his limited focal range. And finally he fell back increasingly on sculpture where at least he could be sure that his sense of touch would always remain true, saying, 'I must learn a blind man's trade now,' although he had in fact always had an interest in modelling.[32]

Among these myopic Impressionists, there is also Pissarro who, unlike his contemporary Degas, had escaped to London before the invading Germans in 1870. He too suffered constant photophobia that forced him to work indoors, often with a patch over the eye.[33] This was evidently due to scarring from corneal ulcers (as Degas may also have suffered), which had plagued him since childhood, distorting the vision and provoking persistent watering (which was attributed to an inflammation of the tear sac). Others to whom myopia has also been imputed include Dufy, Derain, Braque, Vlaminck, Segonzac and Matisse. Among the central European schools of the period we find the same story, for Oskar Kokoschka, Max Slevogt and Emil Orlik are all recorded as having poor vision;[34] indeed, Slevogt 'could not see details at all', and the lack of perspective and depth of the Polish painter Jan Matejko can reasonably be attributed to his myopia, for his spectacles, with − 4 D and − 6 D lenses, have been preserved in the Krakow museum.

Holman Hunt was yet another myope. His spectacles were bequeathed to the museum of the Royal College of Art, but his widow, feeling that myopia was a blemish, apparently went to the length of removing the concave lenses, and inserting weak convex lenses in their place before handing them over.

And lastly in this catalogue we might include Gordon Craig, who was indeed so myopic that Isadora Duncan is said to have complained angrily that he failed to recognize her across the breakfast table. His biographer, Janet Leeper, describes[35] how he 'always loved greys and browns, very low in tone', and the other myopic legacy − the emphasis on structure and loss of detail − is even more a characteristic of his designs (Colour Plate 2).* So it may well have been as an indirect sequel of this myopia that he led a new approach to stage-design, and persuaded his followers of the proper supremacy of colour and form over distracting details; the sets of Reinhardt and Jacques Copeau came naturally in his wake, and this influence is widely apparent today.

In sculpture the same problems confront the myope; short-sighted sculptors tend to concentrate on subjects that can be contained within their limited focal range, and to excel in the

---

*A typical comment is that of the *Times* critic who described the simplicity and severity of Craig's sets for Ibsen's *The Vikings* as 'harmonious in colouring, broad and massive in design'. Craig himself had later recorded how tremendously a flight of steps appealed to him ('when this desire came to me, I was continually designing dramas, wherein the place was architectural, and lent itself to my desire').

His biography also describes how 'in the early days, when Craig was young and unknown, among the few who understood his aim had been the poet W. B. Yeats ... who would discourse on the poetic drama in his vivid magnetic way, peering with myopic eyes into the darkness while Craig was happy to sit and listen to him.' It is tempting to suggest that the vision he so readily shared with Yeats was really a sharing of their mutual dependence on the strange structural world of the myope which Mills so compellingly described (see p. 36).

detailed observation of texture and form. In his biography of Rodin, Rilke[37] describes how 'His myopia was destined to have the most vital influence on his art. Because of his difficulty in

Auguste Rodin The Age of Bronze.

perceiving total effects, his instinct only rarely led him to the composition of monuments on a very large scale, in which the architectural construction is of nearly as great importance as the sculpture proper.' Rodin was accused in his lifetime of having cheated by taking casts of the subjects he was sculpting, since the detail in figures like 'The Age of Bronze' seemed too lifelike to have been wrought otherwise.

So it would seem to be no accident that a survey[38] of the 128 masters and pupils at the Ecole des Beaux-Arts in Paris found 48 per cent to be myopes and 27 per cent hypermetropes, whereas in the population at large it is the hypermetropes who are about three times as numerous as the myopes. Among artists not only does myopia predominate, but such myopic artists, when they cannot manage without their glasses, rarely like having their myopia fully neutralized, and prefer to paint 'undercorrected'.

Myopia and hypermetropia have also been held to have a direct influence on the preponderant colour that artists use. The blue rays of light are refracted more than the red, and so are brought to a focus slightly in front of the normal retina, and the red rays correspondingly just behind it; hence the myope, with his abnormally long eye, will see red objects in better definition, and the hypermetrope, who has an eyeball that is shorter than normal, will have correspondingly better discrimination with blues. This phenomenon has been used as an adjunct for sight-testing in the 'duochrome test'. Indeed, there may be an actual shift of the spectrum in a corresponding direction; thus to the hypermetrope yellow becomes tinged with green, and vice versa. Perhaps even the increasing fascination for reds in the case of Renoir (which has been attributed to incipient cataract) was actually a result of his myopia; and it is a curious coincidence that colours from the red end of the spectrum should play so large a part in the paintings of Chinese and Japanese, who are predominantly myopic (the Japanese have only recently adopted a specific word for blue). Professor Patry[39] once listed a number of Swiss artists whose colours as well as their designs could be readily attributed to their relative hypermetropia or myopia.

Finally, both the myopia and hypermetropia of an artist will have a direct influence on the optimum distance for viewing his work. Artists who record on their rectangles of canvas a relatively small view, normally use a simple geometrical perspective, the laws of which remain approximately accurate only for such a 'narrow-angled' span. Some artists (like Canaletto)[40] achieve a wider-angled effect by basing their geometrical perspective on two points, about 10° apart. Others aim for a more panoramic rendering, after the manner of that eighteenth-century affectation 'the Claude Glass' – a darkened convex mirror in which some (like the poet Gray) preferred to view their landscapes, since it both mellowed the tone and 'opened them out' like a Claude painting.★

A 'Claude Glass'

A darkened convex mirror, which served to mellow the tone and 'open out' the view, widely used by artists in the late eighteenth century.

However, most artists, to a greater or lesser extent, sub-consciously use a 'cylindrical gnomic projection' (such as the conventional Mercator's map of the world) to transpose their view on to a two-dimensional canvas from the surface of the imaginary sphere encircling their heads, on which it seems to be disposed. But the wider the 'angle' of their view, the more

★These convex mirrors were used in all seriousness by the Dutch naturalistic artists of the previous century, sometimes in the form of a crystal ball which is actually depicted in certain of their studies, and this in turn probably derives from their use of one or more mirrors (typically by Vermeer) – a method said to originate with Titian's exploitation of Venetian glass. Gerard Dou is said to have manipulated with his foot a screen in which was set a concave lens bearing a grid of threads to correspond with a similar grid on his canvas. Canaletto, who at sixty-eight was painting distant scenes without glasses, is said to have used a camera obscura (the image of a distant scene being cast through a small aperture into a darkened room on to a screen at close range).

necessary it is to observe the rendering from the same point as that from which it was seen by the original artist who painted it (or camera that photographed it). Even small-angled paintings have their natural distance for correct viewing – corresponding to the radius of that imaginary sphere around the head on to

Photograph showing curves resulting from projection of a wide-angled scene containing a straight line onto flat paper. The balustrade in the foreground is a perfectly straight line in reality.

which the seen world is projected; and for every artist this radius is fairly constant – representing the average distance from his canvases at which he works best. This distance is generally greater for oil paintings than for watercolours, for outdoor paintings than studio paintings, in the long-armed and, most important, in the long-sighted, and the distance is correspondingly shorter in the myope. (This optimum viewing-distance is, of course, related not to the closeness or remoteness of the subject, but only to the canvas, and in vast paintings or murals it is often very great – the artist managing to achieve this by a considerable mental effort, or by frequently stepping backwards, or by working from sketches.)

On this reckoning, A. Wilson[41] has surmised that Vermeer was short-sighted, having a short radius, although placing his subjects at a fair distance away, while Van Gogh similarly had a short radius (and therefore, one hazards, short-sightedness★) but with his subjects at an unusually close range; Van Eyck had a very small radius indeed, while Frans Hals had a larger one, and is therefore a presumptive hypermetrope. Incidentally, almost as a confirmation of this, the preponderance of myopia among miniaturists has already been noted.[42]

★Supported by his childhood habit of walking with half-shut eyes, hunched shoulders, looking at his feet, and being a duffer at ball games.

The Art of the Presbyope

Hypermetropia, or long-sightedness, may thus influence the colours an artist uses and his projection, just as myopia does in the reverse direction. But the principal effect of hypermetropia is shown in the spurious hypermetropia, named 'presbyopia', due to the natural weakness of focusing that comes with middle-age and which causes a progressive difficulty with near-vision. Unless we take to glasses, ordinary reading becomes difficult, and finally impossible, and we can no longer see the details of pictures within arm's range – nor, correspondingly, fashion them.*

It is true that a fuzziness, or what art-historians would call 'breadth', is apparent in the latest paintings of most relatively long-lived artists, such as Rembrandt and Titian. Sometimes artists simply find detailed work too difficult in old age, since as Friedlaender[43] says, ageing artists are often forced to work in a broader way, because their hands, nerves and senses become less responsive (Renoir even tried plastering his paintbrush to his arthritic fingers); and indeed, this may be aggravated by structural damage in the retinas. Thus Michelangelo became nearly blind in old age (wrongly attributed to 'strain' from his exacting work).[44] Piero della Francesca became blind 'through an attack of catarrh' at sixty. Daumier gave up drawing when he was sixty-nine, when he had an unsuccessful cataract extraction. And, because of failing sight, Leonardo's later drawings became less detailed, and he relinquished his fine silver pencil in favour of a red and blue crayon, which he could see more readily. However this frequent change in style may well be attributed in part to a presbyopia that must have rendered the lines on their canvases increasingly ill-defined. For instance Rembrandt's portrait of Saskia, when he was aged twenty-eight, shows the usual delicacy of detail and

*Swift's sorry decline was apparently aggravated by his unwillingness to wear the glasses necessary to compensate for his presbyopia. As Johnson wryly puts it in his *Lives of the Poets*, 'Having thus excluded conversation, and desisted from study, he had neither business nor amusement; for having by some ridiculous resolution or made vow, determined never to wear spectacles, he could make little use of books in his later years: his ideas, therefore, being neither renovated by discourse, nor increased by reading, wore gradually away, and left his mind vacant to the vexations of the hour, till at last his anger was heightened into madness.' It is tempting to add that Adolf Hitler too refused to wear glasses, and documents had to be prepared for him on the large-type 'Führer's typewriter'; but the analogy cannot be stretched too far.

Rembrandt, Portrait of Saskia *(c. 1634).*
An early painting with careful detailing.

Rembrandt, Self-portrait
(c. 1669).
A late work, with loss of detail, attributable perhaps to presbyopia.

Titian, Sacred and Profane Love *(c. 1515–16).*
An early painting with careful detailing.

Titian, The Flaying of Marsyas *(c. 1570).*
A late painting with loss of detail, attributable perhaps to presbyopia.

refinement of feature, in striking contrast to his self-portrait at the age of sixty-three, some months before he died, with the face like a rough-cast in mud. Again, in the early Titians, like *Sacred and Profane Love*, there is plenty of careful detailing, which has all gone by the time we reach a later work like *The Flaying of Marsyas*. This is not to say that such an alteration in style is primarily due to the receding near-point of the artist's clear-vision, but at least this refractive failing may bear something of the blame – or indeed the credit – for this (generally advantageous) change in style.

Astigmatism

As has been said, the eyeball is rarely, if ever, the exact sphere that would permit an ideally clear retinal image. Usually it is a little longer or shorter than optical perfection demands, and the bearer is a little near-sighted or long-sighted in consequence. In addition to this there is nearly always a little flattening of the sphere – usually from above downwards by the pressure of the eyelids, so that the cornea is more curved in that meridian, and vertical lines are less sharply focused on the retina than horizontal lines, or vice versa.

This condition, known as astigmatism, is thus almost universal; and the very slight imperfection of the retinal image in all but the major degrees of flattening causes little, if any, inconvenience. Indeed its existence was hardly recognized until 1825, when Sir George Airy fashioned the first correcting spectacle lens. But those who are abnormally sensitive may find quite small amounts of astigmatism uncomfortable, thus justifying the use of spectacles. It should be added that the eyes can never be 'strained' by overuse or by the effort to clarify a distorted image, and so-called 'eye-strain' is usually the sequel to fatigue or stress projected onto the eye, which is perhaps already congested by tobacco smoke, allergy, etc. But astigmatism is a convenient scapegoat, the spectacles serving primarily as protective screens.* However,

*On the Continent, astigmatism has been described as the 'English disease' because of the British tendency to prescribe very weak correcting lenses, although this may be attributable to the enthusiasm of the vendor, rather than the frailty of the English psyche or an over-sensitivity of the English eye.

when the eyeball is very flattened, particularly in an oblique meridian, these higher degrees of astigmatism can materially confuse and distort the retinal image; and evidence of this can occasionally be recognized in the renderings of such astigmatic artists.

One of the standard sight-tester's methods of assessing astigmatism is to show his patient a chart known as an astigmatic fan. The radiating lines that seem to him least distinct will correspond with the meridian of his least normal corneal curvature. The tester

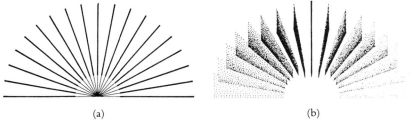

(a)   (b)

(a) 'Astigmatic fan'; *sight-tester's chart bearing radiating lines.*
(b) *The 'fan' as it may be seen by an astigmatic patient, the vertical lines appearing most clear and the horizontal lines progressively less sharply defined.*

can then add neutralizing 'astigmatic lenses' (with their axes corresponding with this meridian) until all the radiations appear equally sharp. Thus an artist with such a degree of astigmatism, who does not wear his glasses (or, as is usual, prefers to have his astigmatic defect undercorrected), might well find, for instance, the horizontal lines to be in clearest focus, and vertical lines least sharply defined; the artist would then tend to emphasize these horizontal lines at the expense of the verticals. One of our most distinguished contemporary artists, Francis Bacon, who had 2 D of horizontal astigmatism, once described how, before the war, he used to paint without glasses; but when he subsequently examined these paintings with his correcting lenses, the vertical brushstrokes 'seemed too coarse, and broken-up, so that the images had lost all their compactness'. Another contemporary, who has a similar astigmatic defect, volunteered that he always tended to draw his vertical lines slightly obliquely, since truly vertical lines seemed to 'shimmer'; and an art student who was recently driven to use such spectacles admitted that the only other way she could get her lines clear was to smoke hashish, but that then she never had enough energy left to paint. Other such artists, especially those with an oblique axis to their astigmatism, rely on correcting the spurious tilts they unconsciously introduce, by checking their paintings in a mirror, where the distortion becomes obvious.

In fact most artists unconsciously emphasize their horizontal lines to indicate the nearness of an object, while emphasis of the vertical lines pushes the object farther away: an optical illusion that is easily demonstrated by drawing a cross and viewing it at

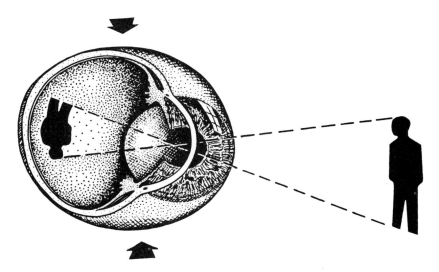

Distortion of image in an astigmatic eye.

different distances.[45] In this way quite a small amount of astigmatism could cause a disproportionate amount of depth-distortion in the rendering. The first reference to the possible influence of an artist's astigmatism was by Liebreich in 1872.[46] He first described a landscape, in the foreground of which some water had been crudely depicted with little horizontal strokes of a different colour, that were quite out of place; and this coarseness was neutralized as soon as Liebreich rendered himself astigmatic by looking at it through an appropriate lens. The second painting he described was a portrait, with an elongation in one meridian which he counted as a sequel to the artist's astigmatic defect, which leads us to the other alleged legacy of an artist's astigmatic eye. Thus, when the eyeball is flattened from above downwards, the retinal image is inevitably a little broader and squatter than the subject it registers.★ This relative elongation is. in fact, extremely slight (about 1 per cent in a moderate degree of astigmatism); nevertheless it forms the basis of the most familiar and time-honoured (albeit the least probable) of all the theories propounding an organic influence on the artist's style, and thus justifies a rather detailed analysis.

The classical instance of an artist whose characteristic style has been (irresponsibly) attributed to an astigmatic eye is El Greco,

El Greco, Portrait of Cardinal Nino de Guevara *(1600)*.

★The reverse is true when such a highly astigmatic artist is actually wearing his glasses, which then cause a slight elongation of the image in the opposite direction (proportional to the distance between the cornea and its correcting spectacle-lens). And one such artist has admitted her need to amend these spurious elongations (rather than any spurious obliquity) in a mirror afterwards.

for in nearly all his paintings there is a vertical elongation, but on a slightly oblique axis, so that all his characters seem to be in danger of sliding off the bottom right-hand corner of the picture. It is interesting to discover how constant, both in degree and meridian, these distortions are when we neutralize them by photographing his paintings through a − 1.0 D astigmatic lens along an opposite meridian (15° off the horizontal). If one looks at the portrait of the Cardinal Inquisitor Nino de Guevara (which has an incidental ophthalmological interest, in that the cardinal is wearing a pair of archetypal spectacles, fastened with a cord

The preceding portrait when photographed through − *1.0* D *astigmatic lens at 15° axis.*

behind the ears in the Chinese fashion), and then at the neutralized rendering of the same painting, one can see that the latter has indeed restored more normal proportions and removed the rather disquieting mal-equilibrium of the cardinal, who had seemed to be slipping off his chair. The same effect is seen in El Greco's painting of Saint Peter and Saint Paul, whose figures again have the tendency to lean or 'glide' to the right, but can be stabilized by the neutralizing lens.

The 'astigmatism' of El Greco seems first to have been suggested in the Paris Medical Chronicle of 1913; thereafter came a desultory and generally sceptical discussion in the European ophthalmic journals,[47] with the Germans generally attacking and the Spaniards protesting. Even in recent years this theory has not lacked occasional advocates.[48]

El Greco, St Peter and Paul *(c. 1592).*

The primary objection to this attribution has always been soundly based on the historical setting of El Greco's work, with his compromise between a Venetian naturalism and an underlying traditional Byzantine stylization, together with the later influence of Tintoretto. All of this is amply supported by X-ray evidence, showing that the elongations were secondarily imposed on his original sketches. But the various advocates and counter-advocates of this theory have seemed more concerned with incidental points, such as the occasional elongation of features, especially hands, when these lie horizontally (as in the portrait of Cardinal Tavera), and the more normally shaped faces of the figures in the foreground of certain paintings (such as *The Burial*

The preceding portrait when photographed through −1.0 D *astigmatic lens at 15° axis.*

of Count Orgaz). Since these foreground figures may represent the donors of the painting, it was thought that they might have required more naturalistic conceptions of themselves, to satisfy their vanity. And so it was argued that El Greco's astigmatism forced him to elongate only when he was drawing imaginary figures – without a 'sitter' to portray, or it could have been that he had one eye that was both astigmatic and far-sighted, while the other was near-sighted and used for close-up figures.[50] Yet others contended that such elongations occurred only when the artist's astigmatism was acquired in advancing age,* as opposed to the normal congenital form.

El Greco was certainly aware of devices for optical elongation, such as the convex mirror used by his fellow-mannerist Parmigianino, who had a similar tendency to vertical elongations. But by far the simplest mechanical explanation of El Greco's distortions derives from the fact that, as a right-handed artist, he would naturally stand rather to the left of his canvas, so as to view the subject, who would be seated beyond its upper left

Holbein, Henry VIII *(1539–40).*

*There is, in fact, a natural tendency for astigmatism to increase during later life along an axis that would promote an increasing vertical elongation. Indeed, enthusiastic supporters of this theory have counted such a natural change as responsible for the style of Gainsborough's later portraits, as well as the increasing elongations of the ageing El Greco.

corner; and that he did not make enough allowance for the tangential spread of its bottom right corner – which necessarily lay at a greater distance from his eye.

Less familiar are the various alleged instances of purely horizontal and vertical elongations. In the well-remembered portrait by Hans Holbein of King Henry VIII, as in many of his other portraits, the figure is broadened, presumably to make it look more portentous; the same portrait can be reduced to more normal human proportions by being photographed through the − 1.0 D astigmatic lens, but on a vertical axis; this suggested that

The preceding portrait when photographed through − 1.0 D astigmatic lens at 90° axis.

Holbein was astigmatic with a vertically compressed eye (as illustrated diagrammatically on p. 51). Some faint support for this theory comes when we note that in portraying his figures recumbent (as in his *Christ in the Tomb*) Holbein generally makes them long and thin, not broad and fat. And there are others, like Rodin, whose squarely built *Burghers of Calais* is attributed to a similar horizontal astigmatism (which is on record, as supplementary to his myopia),[50] and Peter de Wint, whose long, low drawings have provoked the same diagnosis.

Holbein, Christ in the Tomb *(1521);*
and when photographed through $-1.0\,\mathrm{D}$ *astigmatic lens at 90° axis.*

An elongation in a purely vertical meridian is more common, since lissom figures are generally preferred to stumpy ones, and many artists have in their time been lightly categorized as astigmatic,[51] such as Lucas Cranach 'the elder' and even Botticelli and Titian, not to mention even more striking elongators like Modigliani (pp. 60–61). All these suggestions, of course, admit little serious consideration, quite apart from the basic counter-evidence that Modigliani's recumbent nudes and Botticelli's horizontally stretched hands are just as elongated as the upright ones. But in the heyday of these wild attributions, even Cézanne's calculated distortions were declared (in a thesis by Potiron in 1910) to be the product of an astigmatism of 2.5 D at an axis of 45°. Giacometti, the elongations of whose sculptures are clearly beyond any optical explanation, exclaimed, 'All the critics spoke about the metaphysical content or the poetic message of my work. But for me it is nothing of the sort. It is a purely optical exercise. I try to represent a head as I see it.'[52]

Quite apart from the historical and aesthetic reasons that condemn the theory that the shape of the painted image is distorted in proportion to the artist's astigmatism, there is a further natural objection – that the artist paints what he sees, and the subject will correspond to the rendering, however much they are both altered by the misshapen eye into a distorted percept within

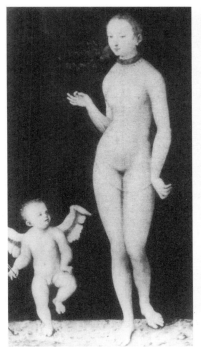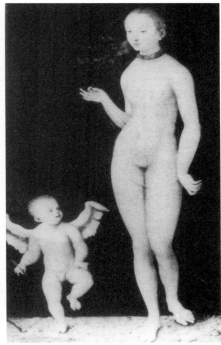

Lucas Cranach the Elder, Lucretia;
and when photographed through − 1.0 D *astigmatic lens at 180° axis.*

the artist's brain. In other words, if he sees a flattened or elongated world, the likeness of it that he puts onto the canvas, in order to appear equally flattened or elongated to him, will in fact be depicted with its proper dimensions restored.

This is essentially, but not entirely, true; for an astigmatic does sometimes, to some extent, distort along the line of his astigmatism. This is easy to confirm by looking through an astigmatic spectacle lens and closing the fellow eye. Then, if we try to draw a circle 'out of our head' (that is, without having one

Modigliani, Portrait of a Girl.

to copy, when we will simply draw its facsimile), the circle becomes elongated along the line of the astigmatism; whereas if we try to draw a line perpendicular to the edge of the paper, this will lean slightly in the opposite direction – presumably because of an intellectual compensation.

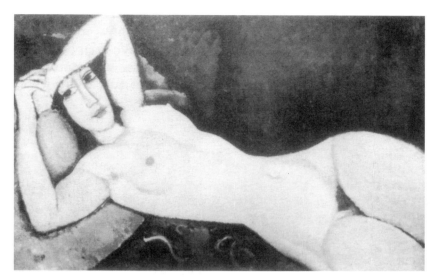

Modigliani, Nude with Raised Arms.

So it is just conceivable that for those of us who tend to assess our worlds haptically (by touch, contour and texture) and kinaesthetically (by the potential for action) rather than visually – in other words, by feeling rather than by sight – an astigmatism might exert some such influence. Thus it could just be argued that the oblique astigmatic, whose retinal images are sloping, but who straightens up his percepts, since his touch and intellect tell him that the objects in fact are upright, may over-compensate when he paints them on his canvas, and the result of this could be that the picture we see is sloping in the opposite direction.

It would perhaps be proper, at this stage, to summarize the relevance of all these theories that attempt to relate the artist's style to his optical aberrations; particularly since such interpretations are always suspect, even to those who do not believe that art has any supernatural or psychoanalytic basis.

It must first be re-emphasized that such an optical distortion is, at the most, only one of many factors that can affect an artist's style, and then only when he is working in a fundamentally naturalistic framework. But, with this proviso, it would seem that the myopic painter, who paints without his glasses and avoids adventitious tricks, such as half-shutting his eyes, using photographs or guesses, and who yet strives for a naturalistic rendering, could reasonably be expected to show some of the changes of form, definition and colour that have been described. The high frequency of myopes among artists, and among the Impressionists in particular, is probably not just coincidental.

Tomb of Salvino d' Armato.
'Inventor of Spectacles, may God forgive him his sins. AD 1317.'

Clearly not all Impressionists were myopic, and there is a vast amount in Impressionism apart from the myopic changes we have noted (such as the intellectual use of complementary colours), but an artist's myopia could indeed have a limited effect on his style.

In the same way the elderly (and non-bespectacled) artist would almost inevitably paint with more breadth, while the rather careless astigmatic might even shift his meridians slightly off-true. And these stylistic changes could contribute to a pattern which the individual artist might then consciously exaggerate, or which his followers could copy.

If we accept this, we may be tempted to wonder how different the world of art might have been if all these famous painters had been forced to wear glasses constantly. We might even agree with Mr Cross, the Vicar of Chew Magna in Somersetshire, who once declared,[53] 'The newly invented optick glasses are immoral, since they pervert the natural sight, and make things appear in an unnatural and a false light,' or with the epitaph in S. Maria Maggiore in Florence which says: 'Here lies Salvino d'Armato, of the Armati of Florence, Inventor of spectacles: may God forgive him his sins. AD 1317.'

=====

CHAPTER TWO

THE ACCEPTANCE OF COLOURS

THE STORY OF THE EMERGENCE of colour-vision is as curious as any in the whole evolutionary saga.

Among the invertebrates, it seems established that certain insects distinguish a variety of colours; indeed their range probably extends far beyond the limited wave-bands of our own visible spectrum, so that they can discriminate 'colour' well out into the ultra-violet – and, for all we yet know, among more distant wave-bands too. But the testing of such awareness is immensely laborious and our knowledge is very limited. Of all other invertebrates, there is little evidence of any differing response to selected wave-bands in the whole electromagnetic spectrum, apart from the crude registration of heat engendered by the infra-red waves.*

But the vertebrate eye, in its earliest known form, had already established a capacity for discriminating between wave-bands from among the small range that corresponds to our own visible spectrum; and throughout the vertebrate stock, the mechanism of this discrimination (as shown by the electrical responses in the optic nerve) remains constant, even though the great majority of vertebrates can evidently make no use of it and are essentially colour-blind. Why we should have decked this limited band of visible light with the panoply of colours as we know them, with

---

*Of the molluscs, even the cephalopods (octopi and cuttlefish), with their highly developed eyes and excellent form-discrimination, seem to have no true colour sense. Among arthropods, the higher crustaceans (such as the lobster) have well-organized eyes comparable to those of their insect cousins, but little sign of colour discrimination, perhaps because they are largely nocturnal in habit; and even the insects are primarily orientated by smell. Although colour-vision varies in different insect species, they generally have a higher response to wave-length changes in the blue to ultra-violet range and, after that, in the red-yellow range; insects also have a unique visual capacity of appreciating changes in the polarization of light.

all their social and aesthetic overtones, is quite another question.

It is true that the physical characteristics of the human eye limit the range, but eyes with tissues that were permeable or responsive to different wave-bands could well have evolved, and there is some evidence that the stickleback fish and the homing pigeon extend their colour discrimination marginally into the ultra-violet region, but to nothing like the degree found in insects. It is also true that waves farther into the infra-red would simply be absorbed by the intra-ocular fluids, but freshwater fish which have a different photo-pigment from our own can see farther into the infra-red.[1] However, the longer the wave-length the larger the diffraction pattern; so, quite apart from chromatic aberrations, it would become impossible in principle to get sharp images. Perhaps we are not missing much on that side of the visible spectrum, as infra-red photography gives us little in the way of a new visual dimension, except in misty weather.

The evolutionary gap is so complete that we are still uncertain from which of the higher invertebrate phyla our vertebrate stock arose (probably it was from some proto-starfish), but from the 'lowest' fishes upwards, the stages are at least clearly signposted. These lowest fishes are still colour-blind, and it is only in the more sophisticated bony fishes – particularly the salmon and trout (as many anglers know to their advantage) – that colour discrimination becomes established. When the vertebrate stock became terrestrial, this faculty was doubtless of little value in the mud of those uncertain streams where the primordial lung-fishes had strayed, and all living amphibia again are essentially colour-blind. So too are all living reptiles with the doubtful exception of certain lizards: again one can see that colours have little relevance in their murky habitat (snakes also make limited use of infra-red sensors). Primitive mammals once more are largely nocturnal or crepuscular; and, even if their successors have often taken to the open plains, they have all, with the single exception of the higher primates, remained essentially colour-blind, so that our domestic animals, whether hunters or hunted, carnivores or herbivores, have a negligible capacity to distinguish hues from the different impulses conveyed up their optic nerve fibres. It should be added that their apparent indifference to colour distinctions is probably comparable to our own relative indifference to refinements of smell, although the absolute sensitivity of the individual smell receptor in man is probably no different to that in the dog; it is just that the dog (having, in any event, a larger olfactory surface within its nose) has learnt to analyse a far greater range of olfactory patterns.[2]

In testing the vertebrates for colour-sense, although a great variety of species has been assessed, one is up against the same practical problems as with the invertebrates, not least in coping with the essential torpidity of fishes and the essential stupidity of birds. Birds have a special system of oil droplets in their retinas, so that they must see, as it were, through yellowish spectacles, and it may be that their blue vision is curtailed in consequence (they also sense magnetic waves). Among mammals, a modicum of colour-discrimination may conceivably exist in squirrels, dogs and horses, but not in their fellow rodents or carnivores or ungulates (bulls being thus quite unaware of red). All lower primates (even the diurnal lemur) are totally colour-blind, even the new-world monkeys have poor red-green discrimination comparable to colour-blind humans. The relative lack of colour in the coats of such mammals, as in amphibia and most reptiles, is complementary to the lack of useful response such colour would provoke.

Only when these vertebrates emerged from the undergrowth and took off into the air as pterodactyls or into the trees as primates did colour-vision return, and all living birds and higher primates can paint their world in colour. For since their trout-like forebears had left the clear river water, they had relied for their orientation on touch and smell, which now were of little avail. At the same time, these birds and primates learned not only to see colours but to evolve the full stereoscopic vision that refines their judgements of distance and space and which is so valuable to ourselves and the birds, but would have been of little benefit to the majority of our earthbound ancestors.

Artistry
in Birds and Mammals
===

Apart from mankind, only two groups of animals seem to have discovered the joys of visual artistry, or at any rate will devote their attention to painting patterns – the Bower-birds and the anthropoid apes. These Satin Bower-birds are rare inhabitants of Australasia, and the darker male bird spends days or even weeks preparing his bower for the enthralled female by painting blue everywhere, stubbing a twig till its ends feather-out into a brush, and using the juices of any blue fruits that it can collect. Blue is indeed a rare colour in nature, so the job is often tedious, and the bird is apparently grateful for any outside help – anything that he can carry he will use, providing only that it is blue – crockery, rags, blue centipedes, bluebells, bus tickets. He will even kill smaller blue birds to make off with their plumage, or snatch a tail-feather from a passing parrot. If one throws a red object, this will be solemnly taken away out of sight of the bower. All this display so dazzles the attendant female that it takes her mind off her primary reason for seeking out the male, and only when the rains come, heralding the seasonal swarm of insects (a diet necessary for the growth of the fledglings), does he stop. Copulation follows, and within a few days these ephemeral paints have all been washed away, and his masterpiece of decoration is gone.[3]

Artistry among the anthropoid apes is more generally familiar, and exhibitions of the masterpieces by certain ape virtuosi have been held in many countries. Some, like Betsy the chimpanzee from Baltimore, have specialized in finger-painting, while the British school under the aegis of Desmond Morris[4] (principally Congo the chimpanzee and Alexander the orang-utan) preferred brushes. And there are many other anthropoid competitors, including a capuchin monkey from Frankfurt, and gorillas from Basel and Rotterdam.

The choice of colour among these anthropoid artists is less easy to assess, since they generally need to have the brush loaded with paint before they will start painting; but Morris noted a definite preference for reds, in so far as they continued using the red-loaded brushes signally longer than those dipped in colours from

The orang-utan Alexander at work on his canvas.

the blue end of the spectrum. And it is tempting to think that, with the evolution of birds, colour-appreciation re-emerged near the blue end of the spectrum, while we anthropoids started re-learning our colours from the opposite spectral end – so that the red paints which Congo found most compelling may well have simply seemed more 'colourful' to him than the blue ones. Or perhaps blue light acts as a tranquillizer (cf. p. 78), dampening

The gorilla Sophie painting.

down the sexual urge in the bower birds, in the same way that red light enhances the passions in birds, as it does in man. Thus we read that there is a farm of white leghorns (in the Essex penitentiary of New Jersey) which prospered only after the birds were fitted with red cellophane spectacles, since otherwise a spot of blood on one hen's plumage always provoked the others to peck her to death.[5] The preference of the young anthropoid artists for daubing with red paint might then be a surrogate for sex, since, as soon as puberty arrived, Congo, the gregarious chimpanzee, started breaking his paint brushes (as if to impress an observer), while Alexander, the solitary orang-utan, simply accepted the proffered brush, together with the keeper's finger, which he bit to the bone.

This apparent preference for red in the higher apes is again echoed in paleolithic cave-paintings, as well as in Greek and Minoan ceramics, although such a colour preference was largely determined by the relative availability of the pigments they used.

The evolution of colour nomenclature in different races is another pointer to the way in which colour-awareness has reached us. In most primitive languages, the colour-names generally refer to colours in the red end of the spectrum, and one word often suffices for the whole of the blue end, from green onwards. Thus the natives of the Carolines have only one name for black, blue and green; among the Swahili, a single word, 'Nyakundu', covers brown, yellow and red, and they now have had to borrow the word 'blue', having no equivalent word of their own; while even in a tongue as sophisticated as Japanese the word 'aoi' sufficed until recently for any colour from green on through the blues and violets.

The same is largely true (as the prime-minister, Gladstone,[6] originally noted in 1858) of classical European languages, in which there is again a striking lack of names for the green–blue range, although there is still some confusion as to the exact hue (or wave-length) that the various names designated. And this essential colourlessness of the blue end of the spectrum (typified by Homer's description of the $\mu\acute{\epsilon}\lambda\breve{\alpha}\nu$ $\ddot{\upsilon}\delta\omega\rho$ – 'black water'*), persists in Italy to this day. Thus Norman Douglas described the difficulty he had in persuading the Calabrian peasants that the Mediterranean was blue; to them and to their forefathers, it had always been black. The confused colour terminology of the Greeks, and the slavish imitation of Greek examples by the Roman poets, have left classical colours as a tantalizing jungle for the lexicographer, but of little real profit to the biologist, physicist or archaeologist.[7]

Finally there is the clinical observation that, in the recovery of sight after cerebral thrombosis, red is always the first colour to intrude – flooding the ill-defined visual scene for a period before the other colours slowly emerge.[8]

If we could persuade ourselves that our spectral range, when rediscovered by the higher apes, started with red, and that they gradually learned to discriminate further and further into the

---

*$o\grave{i}\nu o\psi$, conventionally translated as 'wine-dark (sea)', probably meant dark brown, as also applied to oxen! Aristotle saw only three colours in the rainbow, as did Xenophanes (purple, red and yellow), and Democritus admitted only red and yellow apart from black and white.[7] The *Iliad* omits the colours of flowers and sky, and uses *xanthos* (?yellow) for auburn hair, a chestnut horse and fried fish; *kuaneos* (?indigo) for lion, wood and wet sand (see Appendix 2).

blues, then it would be agreeable to fancy that we humans may continue to colonize our way further down the electromagnetic spectrum, and register as colours more and more of the invisible wave-bands of the ultra-violet, as yet known and enjoyed only by the insects. And, one day, we may even learn to register the wireless waves as colours, and translate sound into a galaxy of extraspectral hues; we already have report of someone who can selectively respond to differing X-ray waves, invisible to the normal eye.[9]

Colour and Temperament

Although the evolution of colour-vision leaves many engaging questions unanswered, it is probable that the emergence of our colour-awareness primarily reflects the establishment of an emotive response to individual colours, rather than any physiological re-orientation. So it is worth examining in more detail this relationship between colour and temperament, that can seemingly determine which of the available colours the brain will be willing to register, and how the mind may yet deploy or distort them to suit the symbolic values that these colours have acquired.

'The rôle of colour in the psychopathological deportment of man is not yet clearly defined': so concludes an analysis by L. Donnet,[10] in a comfortable understatement. The emotive content of colours is indeed a complex issue, but of considerable relevance to all aspects of design; and there have been copious recent investigations based on studies of folklore, the aesthetic or philosophic associations in literature, naturalists' observations (such as the colour imprinting of birds), and the colour-associations in different forms of psychopathology.[11]

Goethe in 1810 first suggested that the human response to colours depended largely on their *biological* cues, reckoning that red, orange and yellow were exciting or enlivening, while blue and purple produced anxious, tender and yearning responses; and, indeed, such biological cues are manifestly important in many animals for provoking their aggression or sexual interest (the stickleback which responds appropriately to the red-tinted belly of an interloper, or the appeal of the blue-behinded ape), as well as for identification of their own young and of appropriate food.★

Apart from providing biological cues, colour responses may be based on *aesthetic* grounds: these are necessarily vague and various, and depend not only on individual colour associations, but on combinations involving colour-contrast, complementaries and mixtures, to admit a complexity that has daunted most investigators.

Finally, colours provoke because of their *symbolic* content. Broadly speaking, these are either acquired or instinctive. Their 'acquired' significance is largely arbitrary, depending on traditions and education: thus the Devil is usually black in Western cultures, and red in the Far East; purity is signified by white in the West and saffron in the East, mourners wore white in ancient Greece, wear purple in Turkey and black in the West; and a bevy of recent political and religious groups have established their own colour-labels. Certain of the 'instinctive' attributes are more fixed, such as those that depend on simple tactile influence: thus red is almost inevitably a hot colour suggesting fire and blood, and blue/mauve is cold. Others are less established – such as the green of plant-life suggesting growth and 'organic serenity', and yellow, the colour of gold, suggesting royalty (and God the Father). To which may be added a host of alleged associations that are based only on an arbiter's caprice or some metaphysical dogma.

Thus the four spectral bands – red-orange, yellow-green, blue-indigo and violet – are respectively Bilious, Nervous, Phlegmatic and Sanguine if one accepts the Hippocratic divisions; or Phosphoric, Fluoric, Carbonic and Sulphuric, for those who fancy the 'constitutions' of the homeopath. In psychometric terms the red-

---

★Goethe complained that Newton had reduced the glory of colours to the purely physical, a view he repeated in lines from *Faust*:

> Grey, dear friend, is all theory,
> And green is the golden tree of life.

In fact, Newton was just being cautious, since he closed his first paper with the words:
'To determine ... by what modes or actions light produceth in our minds the phantasms of colours is not so easie. And I shall not mingle conjectures with certainties.'

green bands are said to favour the introvert, and the blue-violet the extrovert.

Even apart from these antiquated systems, the relationship between personality and colour preferences fully retains its fascination for psychologists today. For instance, it has been established that we tend to remember colours as redder or greener than they really are,[12] and this bipolar hue-shift may conceivably stem from some instinctive preference.

An insight into the preferences of nursery-school children was gained by telling them respectively sad and happy stories, and asking them to draw a portrait of the girl around whom the story centred. It was then found that the 'sad' group used a brown crayon to colour her dress, and the 'happy' group used a yellow crayon, implying that colour-mood exists at a very early age. Another analysis[13] showed that male students were consistent and uniform in their order of colour preference, while women were consistently inconsistent. As early as 1921 Rorschach[14] had described the colour-relevance of the ink-blots whose value in personality assessment he had already established, assessing these in terms of impulsivity, suggestibility and emotionality. Recent research has made extensive use of the coloured blots of the Rorschach test, finger painting and the colour-pyramid tests. Others[15] have expanded the field by analysing the subjects' preferences among a wide range of tartans, but the results are largely contradictory or indecisive, apart from indicating that there is a generally reduced use of colour by depressives (which one might indeed have guessed at the start).

In schizophrenia, where the whole perceptual world becomes very impoverished, all colours tend to fade in the overwhelming bleakness of the scene. Paintings by schizophrenics betray little change in their colour symbolism, although the colour combination of black and red has repeatedly been observed in patients with suicidal tendencies, and those with acute psychosis often paint in monochrome. To this general rule, Van Gogh is in part an exception, perhaps because his depression stemmed from a different source.[16] Suggested diagnoses have included cerebral tumour, syphilis, magnesium deficiency, temporal lobe epilepsy, poisoning by digitalis (given as treatment for the epilepsy, which could have provoked the yellow vision), and glaucoma (some self-portraits show a dilated right pupil, and he depicted coloured haloes around lights). During his last summer he painted 'immense expanses of wheat beneath troubled skies', and after completing the last of these – a storm-tossed cornfield, out of which an ominous flight of crows was rising – he shot himself, clumsily but fatally, telling his would-be succourers not to try to save his life as 'the sadness will last for ever'.[17] (Colour Plate XIII).

Illness, fatigue and despair often tend to make the world seem, literally, less colourful – like a deepening narcosis. Thus deafness, which causes a personality to withdraw from life and the warmth of human contact, is said to render everything down to a melancholy grey; and this is not just an emotional change, for profoundly deaf children have been found to have significantly lowered colour discrimination.[18] A recent patient who exclaimed, 'Deafness takes all the colour out of things,' spoke for a myriad of his less articulate fellow-sufferers. Goya, after an illness at forty-seven, became deaf for the remaining thirty-five years of his life,★ and all the gaiety and colour was lost from his paintings, as the subjects became distressing and often horrifying; just as Swift's writings became more venomous as his deafness grew ever more intense.[20]

Poetic Colour Imagery

In seeking to understand the symbolic relevance of different colours, some have explored the colour-imagery of some of our major poets. Any interpretation of their findings is inevitably rendered less secure by the many factors involved; for often poets, like artists, merely have private individual preferences, and these may change with the mood of the poet as well as with advancing age. Nevertheless it is of some value to discover whether any material differences in the overall use of colour and choice of hues can be related to the idiosyncrasies or the temperamental approach of the individual poet.

★Goya's deafness was associated with partial blindness and a transient hemiplegia, suggesting the diagnosis of an obscure disorder called Vogt-Koyanagi Syndrome, and not (as often quoted) due to syphilis or poisoning from lead after licking his paintbrushes.[19]

In a fairly extensive survey, E. Slater[21] found that Milton, Marlowe, Poe, Arnold, Browning and Shakespeare were all very sparing in their use of colour. Shakespeare and Marlowe indeed used less colour and more sombre colours in their dramas than in their poems. And when Chapman completed one of Marlowe's unfinished poems (*Hero and Leander*), although he retained much of Marlowe's style, colour-names kept tumbling in. On the relatively rare occasions when Milton used colour images, specifically mineral names (like gold) tended to predominate.

Of the poets who used copious colour-images, Shelley and Keats were to the fore, Shelley generally using straightforward and commonplace colour-names (like yellow, blue, purple, green, etc.), whereas Keats preferred to relate his colours to other (usually tactile) images (like damask, verdurous, Tyrian, rubious, argent). This tendency is still more evident with other colourists such as Gerard Manley Hopkins, and especially with Francis Thompson whose colour-images include: the crocean and amethystine lustre, amaranthine weed, greening sapphire sea, rubied sun, ruby-plumaged flames, pearled moon, a ribbed track of cloudy malachite, metallic vapours, burnished sun, clarified silver, golden bars (golden and silvery appear very often).

Of the specific hues, most poets preferred reds and other 'warm' colours, Thompson having a rare affection for browns, while Matthew Arnold had a penchant for whites (silver, snow, milk, moon-silvered, moon-blanched); only Edward Lear, Coleridge and Shelley seemed to favour blues and greens.

Slater concluded that the total extent to which colour is used correlates positively with the sensory or eidetic qualities of the poet's mind, and negatively with his tendency towards the abstract. Thus Browning, Milton and Shakespeare are of an intellectual stamp compared to Shelley, Keats and Thompson, who are poets of feeling. The qualitative difference (preference for reds or greens) really showed little personality or temperamental influence.

The issue is, of course, complicated by the distinction that must be made between the 'natural' colours recorded in poetry and the 'artificial' colours referring to heraldry, embroidery, jewellery or even to the four humours and other half-forgotten systems of pre-scientific eras. In the Middle Ages naturalism had barely emerged, and most of the poet's colour-images seem to emanate from a medieval tapestry. Even in the time of Shakespeare colours were still being used in a stylized way, as if in a device, and sometimes assumed not only an emblematic but almost a moral quality (e.g. *The multitudinous seas incarnadine, making the green one red*).

Synaesthesia

But in the universality of art, the emotive significance of colours knows no bounds. If colours can be abstracted from their natural lights and pigments, and turned into the emblematic or symbolic labels of the poets' images, they can be further abstracted to embellish the very letters and syllables with which the words are framed. To Rimbaud each of his vowels symbolized an individual colour, which he immortalized in his poem 'Voyelles' (see Appendix 3). And the early-nineteenth-century author/musician, E. T. A. Hoffman, explained, 'It is no mere image or allegory, when the musician says that colours, scents and light-rays appear to him as musical sounds, that their blending is to him a magnificent concert.' Such a 'colour-hearing', every sound being associated with its special colour, is no isolated phenomenon; it is probably commoner than we believe, because such people may have little occasion to mention these associations, which to them may seem quite normal and even pleasurable, and which, in any case, may be difficult to explain to their fellows. It usually starts in early childhood, along with the discovery of language; the colours tend to become brighter as the pitch ascends, and the pattern may become so elaborated that every sentence is lit by a brilliant display of coloured lights. The artist Kandinsky had it that the shades of blue, from pale to dark, correspond to a timbre-scale descending from the flute, through the cello and double-bass to the organ; and there has been a report[22] of a patient for whom all sounds, whether spoken or musical, had an attendant colouring; it is interesting that two of her vowel-colours in fact corresponded with those which Rimbaud had recorded, although it appears inconceivable that she had ever read 'Voyelles'.

The translation of sound into colour is also familiar in classical music. Rimsky-Korsakov felt that each tone had its own specific colour (c = white, d = green, etc.). Arthur Bliss composed a 'Colour Symphony', labelling the four movements respectively purple, red, blue and green, based on the symbolic associations of these colours in heraldry (see Appendix 3), and Scriabin created his *Prometheus, a Poem of Fire*, with a 'keyboard of light' from a colour-organ, that underscored the intensity of the magic he wished to project. In fact this proved rather a failure, largely through the purely mechanical scheme whereby the light was made to 'duplicate' dully the chordal outline of the orchestral score. But the idea was soon commercialized; and 'colour-sound' and 'white-sound' devices, which projected kaleidoscopic or snow-fall patterns on a screen to synchronize with musical tapes, were marketed as a social distraction, or as an 'analgesic' that found a limited use in dental surgeries and other situations where apprehension could be cloaked by such a blunderbuss sensory impact.

This spilling-over from one of our senses into another was first described by J. T. Woolhouse, the engaging royal groom who became oculist to James II and William III, among his blind patients, and these 'synaesthesias' can indeed overlap the senses in all directions. Thus it has been known (since 1669) that the partially deaf can hear better in the light than in the dark, and spectacles have even been recorded as an aid to hearing.[25] The acuity of vision may apparently be improved by both high and low auxiliary sound stimuli.

The 'memory-man' recently described by A. R. Luria[23] suffered an almost total recall because of the diffusion of his synaesthesias. With every sound he experienced light, colour, and often taste and touch. The memory of a fence that he had passed on his walk was fixed because, as he explained, 'it has such a salty taste and feels so rough . . . it has such a sharp, piercing sound'.

The Influence of Environmental Colour

We have tried to assess the *intrinsic* relevance of different colours in the individual, both as a passive reflection of his temperament and as actively deployed in his poetic expression. The *extrinsic* relevance of colours, the effect on our behaviour of the colour of our environment, is happily a far simpler issue. Indeed, the commercial incentive of interior decorators, stage designers and couturiers has given it more of an airing than it probably deserves.

It is generally accepted that the colours from the red end of the spectrum are stimulating and warm, while the blues and greens are relaxing and cool (cf. p. 68). W. E. Miles[24] reports that in one café the women employees found that they could discard their coats when the blue walls were repainted orange; and the sedative value of blue colours is used to advantage in hospitals, particularly when dealing with the emotionally disturbed. The stimulating effect of red has been shown to facilitate the muscular responses in a group of students whose reaction-time was accelerated when they were exposed to red instead of green illumination, and at the same time their estimates of the passage of time were increased as the lighting changed from blue towards red.

Yellow is a more capricious colour: certain shades can predispose to nausea, and are wisely avoided in the interiors of aircraft, or even in the food served on air or ocean voyages, while another shade of yellow has been used in decorating classrooms in order to improve the work of the schoolchildren.

The darkness of colour also gives an illusion of weight: Miles reported how workmen in a factory stopped complaining of the weight of the black boxes they were required to lift when these were repainted bright green.

Interior decorators are great individualists, but a few generalizations are permissible concerning the colours recommended in our homes. Thus it is common to provide a bluish bedroom in order to relax the spirit and lower the blood-pressure, a salmon-coloured bathroom to give the best 'rosy' glow to the exposed flesh, a peach-coloured dining-room to foster the appetite (this is said to be further enhanced if augmented by another edible colour, such as lettuce-green or apple-red); and for the drawing-room, since one's eyes are first attracted to brightness, the furniture can be displayed to the best advantage against a soft and dark background hue.

Crying infants can be more readily quietened by blue light than by red, for after only fifteen days from birth some crude colour-discrimination is possible.[25] Film stars have been known to demand a background colouring to suit every mood of their exacting rôles (red for romance, blue for reflection, and so on). And the choice of colouring in clothing, cars and all the other appurtenances of living is clearly a vast issue, which this is no occasion to explore.

Therapeutic Use of Colour

Finally, colour has been used as a therapy, not just as a tranquillizer or a psychological adjuvant, but in the firm belief of its mastery over disease. Just as John Gaddeston cured the son of Edward I by wrapping him in a scarlet coat, as a specific protective against smallpox, yellow has been the traditional treatment for eye-disease, since the use of disembowelled frogs by the Assyrians, and of bile by Tobias, up to the recent ocular panacea, Golden eye ointment.[26] Urine remained a standard eye-lotion till replaced by amber ale, by Walter Bayley, physician to Queen Elizabeth I, who counted it more effective for 'strengthening the sight'.

Green light is traditionally life-enhancing. For the ancient Egyptians this belief is said to have derived from the colour of the Nile in its July floods; the serenity we experience from country views perhaps stems from the same archetypal source. Pliny recorded that tired eyes could be restored by looking at green objects; and the emerald through which Nero used to watch his lions eating the Christians perhaps served to temper that lurid scene.

Early spectacles were often sea-green in colour, being some-times made from beryl (hence, it is argued, the German word for spectacles 'Brille'[27]), since it was believed that such a precious stone enhanced the benefit from the colour, as in the use of malachite for the treatment of cataract enjoined by the Ebers Papyrus[28] of 1500 BC.★

In those early days colour filters provided an acceptable compromise between the damaging effects of strong light and

★A 'Really excellent' treatment for cataract entails the insertion of malachite, pounded with honey, while incanting: 'Come Malachite, Come Thou Green One. Come discharge from Horus' eye. Come Secretion from Atun's eye ...'

Since all colours had, to early civilizations, a supernatural quality, the Ebers Papyrus contains a host of other such formulas, recommended because of the colour of their ingredients.

darkness. Xenophon had described snow-blindness, and blindness from sun-gazing was recorded by Lucretius.[29] ('The sun, too, blinds ... because his power is great, and the idols from him are borne through the clear air, sinking heavily into the deep, and strike upon the eyes, disordering their texture.') The bizarre view that darkness could equally be damaging was even held by the Venerable Bede;[30] he may have borrowed this from Isidorus, a seventh-century bishop of Hispalis in Spain, who declared in his book of Origins: 'nox a nocendo dicta, eo quod oculis noceat' (night was so named from the harm it did to the eyes).

Even today the therapeutic value of colour is far from obsolete, although more discreetly acclaimed: the great flasks, filled with water in traditional chemists' shop-windows, the pink aspirin to deceive the regular white-aspirin taker and, not least, the various tinted spectacle lenses that so many of our citizens are persuaded to buy – nearly always having no clinical justification.

Dream-Colours

It is sometimes argued that dreams are like old films, without sound or colour, and that colour is only imposed later, as in tinting a black-and-white picture; or else that we normally dream in colour, but the memory traces of colour are subsequently bleached out.[31]

The relevance of colour in dreams remains conjectural, but we now know that dreaming in the adult occurs during a cyclically recurring sleep pattern, characterized by electrical activity in the brain, and by rapid movements of the eye; which are apparently associated with the nature of the hallucinative visual imagery of the dream. These rapid eye movements, noted long ago by Aeschylus,[32] are rare in the deeper stages of sleep, when dreaming itself is also rare.[33] They are nearly always accompanied in males by penile erection except when the dreams are compounded with anxiety,[34] in which case the dreams also tend to be decolourized. An increase in the intensity of dream-colours is usually noted by the recently blind, who often relish (and are impatient to resume) these dreams that recreate their lost visual world.[35]

Such dreaming occurs in about 20 per cent of adult human sleep, and has also been demonstrated in the monkey, cat, mouse and opossum (which, like the newborn baby, spends most of its twenty-four hours asleep). In premature babies an ill-defined sleep-state at thirty-one weeks leads to a more specific sleep at thirty-seven weeks, when the rapid eye movements can first be recorded (associated with shallow, rapid and irregular breathing, raised pulse, etc.). It is suggested that dreaming has simply been grafted on to these rapid eye movements, which are controlled by the vegetative part of the brain (rhombencephalon) and have some primitive vital function.*

Speculations on the significance of dreams abound in history; but the first reasoned appraisals followed the writings of Freud at the opening of this century, and traditional psychoanalysts still interpret every dream and its colour-range in sexual terms that may amuse or astonish the unprepared lay mind. Thus the dream-screen on which the colours are deployed is said to represent the infantile visual perception of the female breast, and the presence of the colours are then said to indicate 'repressed anal excremental contents', on the grounds that colour-interest receives special impetus during the 'anal phase' of development,[37] and the colours thus expose one's repressed scotophile or exhibitionist tendencies. The specific colour is said to relate to its symbolic associations (red = blood, penis, sexual prohibitions, etc.; white = virgin, purity; green = permissiveness, youth and so on).

This alleged symbolic meaning of colour in our dreams can be paralleled in its use by artists. Thus Van Gogh's use of yellow is considered to derive from the sun,[38] and appears to be related to an ambivalence to his father, as expressed in sun-worship, while the complementary colours red and green were correlated with his bisexuality and castration anxiety.

Colour in art can also establish identity – of the individual artist (like Tiepolo) who has a personal colour-style, which can serve as a signature; or it can indicate the sex, as in Egyptian art, where the male bodies were painted red and the female ones yellow.

*To Crick, this REM sleep is a method of clearing up our unconscious dreams, hence their frequency in children and their hallucinatory nature.

In waking life, these rapid eye movements are also evident during 'active' thinking, when objects are imagined to be moving, and on suppression (as opposed to generation) of a wish.[36]

Repetitive colour dreams are said to be related to traumatic events accompanied by a visual shock in which colours were involved, or defensively incorporated on a screen; and it is considered that successful artists simply learn to re-project this scene in its associative colours.

Various surveys[39] have attempted to give statistical answers to the question of degree and frequency of dream-colours. One conclusion from these is that recognition of dream-colours is relatively rare, commoner in women and children, and more often mentioned spontaneously by women and by neurotics; in fact it is reckoned that, just as we rarely take note of specific colours in daily life, since we are essentially concerned with what things *mean* for us, colour is not important in our conceptual thinking in light sleep.

Simpler theories exist, which might seem very naïve to psycho-analysts, but have a certain elementary appeal. For instance, some have observed that, as we are surfacing fairly slowly from a dream, we seem to traverse a colour-threshold, and these colours – usually blues and greens – may flood in to ravish us, before we finally awake, with only the memory of a vivid experience left to clutch at, before it drifts back into the underworld of our Id. So it might be argued that, since colour-vision was a very recent re-acquisition in our ascent through the mammalian evolutionary tree, it is among the first attributes to be lost as we sink more deeply into sleep, and to return only at the last moment as we re-emerge from the depths. And it then strikes us with the same vividness and freshness that it strikes the mind of the child (who, in his individual life, is recapitulating our human evolutionary ascent).

The gradient of our sleeping and awakening is difficult to adjust; but controlled sleep under narcosis affords some support for this fanciful theory – that colour-vision, as a late-comer in our evolution, is possible only in the 'lightest' of sleeps (when consciousness is not far away), and is quickly lost, along with our higher cerebral functions, as we descended to the primordial animal-self, which alone continues to function in our deepest sleep. Thus as one descends under the influence of ether from the level of the 'directed reverie' into the 'dream-like phase' – the figures of one's dream-drama may shrink in size but the colours become richer and vitalized, generally restricted to primary or secondary colours, yellows, greens and blues, but only very rarely reds (just as is true with mescaline-narcosis, and indeed with natural dreams).[40] As these figures often seem stereotyped and segmented by heavy black lines between the coloured patches, the effect is that of a painting by Rouault, or of a stained-glass window, and the spell they may cast has a religious intensity – in

Rouault, The Old King *(1916–36).*

the same way that the figures described by one patient as he emerged from a mescaline overdose had the postures and the compelling intensity of Old Testament prophets, with the Jehovah coming straight out of a Blake illustration. Finally, as the narcosis deepens, the colours ebb away, and a grey mist covers all.

===

CHAPTER THREE

THE WITHDRAWAL OF COLOURS

ALTHOUGH, IN GENERAL TERMS, all mankind can discriminate between the full range of spectral colours, a surprisingly large minority have very restricted colour-awareness of certain parts of this spectrum – nearly always in the red and green areas. To these, red and green largely appear as grey, unless their colouring is very brilliant. There are degrees and varieties of such colour-blindness. To some, red and green are barely distinguishable from one another; to some it is specific-ally the red or the green that is apparently 'decolourized', while to a very small group the blues and yellows are primarily affected; and an even smaller group sees all colours with such diminished intensity that they live in the essentially monochrome world of their mammalian forebears.

Colour-blindness is a curious sex-linked hereditary defect, affecting about one in twelve men and less than one in 200 women, almost irrespective of race or geography. It is readily disclosed by looking at book-plates in which coloured spots form patterns that are specifically misinterpreted by colour-defectives (Colour Plate III).

The frequency of red-green colour-blindness seems to rise in proportion to man's distance from his primitive state, with the lowest rate in the aborigines of Australia, Brazil, Fiji, North America and among the Mongols[1] and the highest rate in Europe and the East, including the Brahmins of India. A possible expla-nation of this is that colour vision is less important for survival in a civilized society.[2] For the same reason, perhaps, and especially where interbreeding permits this recessive gene to become more manifest, the proportion of colour-defectives is much higher; thus, among Quakers,[3] it was nearly double the normal per-centage (although this has also been explained as the result of a breeding-out of true artists from a group 'who counted the fine arts as worldly snares, whose most conspicuous practice was to dress in drabs'). Another survey[4] has shown that, if one travels down a line from Aberdeen to Plymouth, there is a progressive increase in the frequency of colour-defective males – for which no explanation is forthcoming.

The very rare recessive gene that yields total colour-blindness is remarkably constant in frequency among different races, becoming manifest in about 1/30,000 of the population of Europe and of Japan. It becomes rather more frequent only in enclaves where consanguineous marriages are common.

No specific personality changes have been established for these colour-blind minorities (except for a tendency to be more extro-verted and less neurotic); it has also been noted how criminals were readily divisible into the bright and emotional and the sombre and observant, and that the same division existed among schoolboys, with the colour-defectives all belonging to the sombre minority.[5]

The distortion of normal colour-values is very striking, but since it is so hard to compare the colours that we see with those seen by another, the very existence of colour-blindness (although surmised by the ancient Greeks) was not established until 1798, when the chemist Dalton discovered that he himself was red-green colour-blind, and labelled the condition 'Daltonism'.*

The influence of colour-blindness on industry and the pro-fessions is well-recognized today, and stringent tests are now undertaken for train-drivers, pilots, naval officers and electricians (since colour-coding of the cables is generally used); perhaps as a consequence there is a high proportion of colour-defectives in the Royal Marines (? rejects from the Navy), just as there is among engravers (who were perhaps artist-rejects), although colour-blind engravers have looked on this finding as a tribute to the ease and precision with which they select the relative tone cor-responding to each colour in nature.[7]

---

*He bequeathed his eyes to Dalton Hall in Manchester, hoping – in the blithe mechanistic manner of his generation – that the anatomist who dissected them would discover a simple colour-filter which would explain all. Adequate preservatives were not then known, so his shrivelled eyeballs are still waiting to be opened.[6] Although Dalton claimed the 'discovery', colour defects were first recorded by Huddart in a Cumberland family thirty years earlier.

In earlier days there must have been many problems for the colour-defective apprentices in illumination and mosaics. In 1870 Francis Galton[8] discovered that there were 40,000 bins of mosaic stones still in the Vatican that might have shed some light on this problem; but, by 1886, when 10,752 had already been classified, his investigation had to be dropped because the price asked by the Vatican became excessive.★

Only occasionally in industry are the colour-defectives sufficiently high in the establishment for their distorted colour-values to make much impact. One alleged instance is the case of 'Stroudley's Improved Engine Green', a paint adopted by certain railway companies of which Stroudley was superintendent, which was actually golden; he was said to have just been unaware that he was a 'green-defective'.

Colour-Blindness in Literature and Art

The influence of colour-blindness on literature is little evident, since writers and poets vary greatly in their use of colour, as was noted earlier; and the colour-defective writer will simply be thought casual in his use of colour-names, when, in fact, his genes have left him little option in the matter. There is, however, one poet – Berend Jentsch – whose colour vocabulary attracted enough attention to court the label of a red-green defective, a diagnosis subsequently shown to be correct. An analysis of forty of his poems revealed that he used the word blue nine times, yellow seven times, green, grey, black and white three times, and red only once.

★Mosaic material includes a limited variety of naturally coloured 'stones', and the large majority are 'smalti' – glass with the addition of various metallic oxides as opacifying and colouring agents, which permit an almost infinite number of shades. Their exact chemical constitution, which differs from factory to factory, is usually kept secret.

The Vatican mosaic studio of the 'Reverenda Fabbrica de S. Pietro' was established in 1727, with a factory that was in existence until early this century; and the tesserae they are using now are still largely drawn from this enormous stock (28,000 varieties apparently remain available). This incredible number reflects the earlier fashion of using mosaics to imitate the colour gradations of natural painting as closely as possible, rather than the current boldly juxtaposed tesserae of widely different colours which, as in pointillism, will, it is hoped, merge on the retina.

Within a few years of Dalton's discovery, Goethe[9] discussed the possible effects of colour-blindness on artists (such as Uccello). This was elaborated by Liebreich[10] who, at 'The London Exhibition' in 1871, noted how certain painters depicted roof-tops and oxen (popular contemporary themes) as red when on the well-lit side, and as green when on the dark side. That this so-called 'Sign of Liebreich' characterized the red-green colour-blind, was confirmed by subsequent writers. In 1908 Professor Angelucci[11] exhibited paintings by three colour-defective artists in Naples, particularly remarking how one artist, who had depicted a naked child wholly in green, since it was sitting in the shadow, admitted that red and pale green both seemed grey to him. Angelucci also remarked how the tree leaves, when lit by the sun, were not yellow-green but bright yellow, and those in the shade were blue-green or sometimes entirely blue.

Albertotti,[12] who disputed Liebreich's findings, used as his yardstick the manner in which the artists painted a rainbow, and counted as colour-defective only those who used two or at the most three colours. But with some artists who used limited colours (such as Constable, Turner and Millet), he admitted that they might have limited themselves to rendering only the dominant tones, since the infinite colour-gradations could not truly be recalled. Broschmann[13] reckoned that colour-defective artists started by frankly distorting their colour-values, and later on they learnt how best to compensate, but still made mistakes in the details.

It seems that colour-blind painters, particularly those with a rather recessive temperament, generally try to compensate for their failing by reducing the colour-content of their pictures, which often seem a little melancholy in consequence (as in Colour Plate VII). Whistler is an alleged example of this, and so is Carrière, who depicts his faces dimly emerging from his paintings like ghosts from the darkness. Grottger,[14] the Polish master of pencil and charcoal, is another and well-established instance, since he conceded that colours were right out of his reach; and Meryon, who ranks with Piranesi among the greatest of architectural engravers, evidently abandoned painting because of defective colour vision (he later relinquished even engraving, and retired to an asylum, believing that he was Christ).

However, a minority of colour-blind artists (generally those with a more dominant personality) prefer to use exalted colours, but keep clear of the ambiguous reds and greens, and avoid intermediate shades, tints and hues which they would find hard to distinguish, and which in any event appear to them rather uninteresting and irrelevant. In this category Fernand Léger has been quoted as well as Mondrian, with his preference for a primary red, yellow and blue, with avoidance of green. Several famous living painters and at least one art critic are known to be red-green colour-blind; while it was said by the oculist who attended Paul Henry that his established red-green colour-defect was responsible for the blue mountains, white cottages and silver-white clouds that were such a feature of his Irish landscapes (Colour Plate VI). It has even been argued that Constable was partially red-green colour-blind and therefore needed to use additional red in building-up his green matches.[15] Certainly his paintings often look autumnal – Fuseli once wrote to Wilkie, 'I like the landscape of Constable, but he always makes me call for my greatcoat and umbrella' – yet Constable himself declared in 1833: 'I never did admire the autumnal tints, even in nature ... [but] I love the exhilarating freshness of spring.' Some of Constable's pictures are indeed far from autumnal in colouring, with the blue-greens predominant and white light sparkling in the foliage, but this would be a natural change in any red-green colour-defective artist (because of his high 'luminosity-curve') if painting in a pale sunlight instead of the usual overcast English day.

Doubtful support to this theory is also lent by Constable's own comments on the paintings of his contemporaries, which he was apt to describe as insipid or vapid, since he perhaps saw the greens as pale or fawn-coloured (conceivably because they lacked the extra dose of red that he himself would have inserted). He described Farington's landscapes as 'heavy and crude' but added pertinently that they looked much better by twilight, perhaps because the natural colour-shift of vision in fading light would have made the red pigment that Farington had used in his greens seem to him darker.

This theory of Constable's colour-defect is interesting, but does not take into account the attitude of artists in Constable's day to the use of colour. Corot once said that drawing comes first, then tone and colour last; and to help distinguish brightness contrasts (= tone) he used a 'Claude glass' (p. 43) in order to exclude the colour content. Brown trees were a standard feature of contemporary paintings: as Sir George Beaumont remarked to Constable, 'A good picture, like a good fiddle, is always brown, and one should always include a brown tree in every landscape.' (This so provoked Constable that he picked up a fiddle and laid it on the lawn, to demonstrate the contrast.) And if it surprises us that Constable should have told Sir George that he 'never put such a thing [as a brown tree] into a picture', we must not forget the even browner trees of his predecessors. Indeed, the majority of Constable's paintings are yet uncleaned, so that some of his apparently dark pigments are simply the result of a browning of the varnish.

One way of investigating the effect of colour blindness is to provide a painting for a known colour–defective artist to copy or, if he was not much of an artist himself, simply to try to match from his paint-box the colours he saw onto a sheet of paper with the correct outlines already pencilled-in. Two such illustrations by patients of Dr Lanthony[16] (Colour Plates IV and V) nicely illustrate the confusions usually made by colour-defectives; the copy of Van Eyck's 'Mystical Lamb' exhibits the common inversion of red-orange and yellow-green, the blues being more or less correct; in the copy of Gauguin's 'Ta Matete' by one with dulled awareness of green (a 'deuteranomalous'), the colours of the dresses are shifted in the direction of green, yellow becoming greenish, red-orange becoming yellow.

A number of colour-blind artists have been investigated during recent years; and of one, Donald Purdy, who exhibited the classic failings and compensations of the red-green colour-defective, R. W. Pickford[17] has given us this detailed report:

His early work was in dull colours. In the middle phase he followed the kind of colour scheme characteristic of the Barbizon painters, with a predominance of greys and browns. In the latest phase he had come to exploit brilliant colours in juxtaposition. He said that any 'transparent' colours would go together, and that he was always aiming at 'transparency' of effect. He asked whether brilliant colours were not very tiring to look at, producing nervous exhaustion and said that he found painting with

brilliant colours both exciting and fatiguing. He had developed the technique for using brilliant colours because he found that prospective buyers
liked the paintings done in this way.

It was apparent that he tends to make the structural parts of his paintings
in blues, browns, oranges or yellows, and that he put in reds, purples and
greens incidentally. He said that he found reds the most exciting of colours,
but the 'reds' which he used, and to which he referred, were usually
subdued or brownish. He pointed out that in his view other people,
and especially prospective buyers, do not like 'red-and-green' paintings,
because they are 'Christmassy', like paintings of robins and holly. His own
greatest preference is for blueish greens and brownish colours.

Mr Purdy proved to be a simple 'deuteranomalous' or partially
green-blind subject; he consequently saw as yellowish all colours
that were greenish to the normal-sighted, finding a 'pure green'
only among the blue-green shades. Yellows tended thus to appear
to him more orange, and oranges as redder than they would to
the normal eye. In the same way, he called a sky-blue 'lilac', and
for red he chose a purple pigment. He said he was particularly fond
of 'reddish-greens' – a term Pickford had previously recorded as
peculiar to the deuteranomalous.[18]

The particular interest of this artist is that he started out tending
to avoid bright colours (like Whistler, Grottger and Carrière) and
then, having been reluctantly persuaded to join the dominant
group, over-compensated by the introduction of bold colours,
which he could poorly assess, but which he felt his public required.

Pickford subsequently reported two further artists[19] – one who
was red-blind and used quiet colours, and one, partially red-blind,
who used bold colours, the difference being largely conditioned
by temperament. Thereafter, he collected nine colour-defective
art-students who confirmed the influence of temperament. The
bold ones, ignorant of their defect or insensitive about its presence,
tend to use colours in a striking way that may seem original; the
sensitive ones seek self-consciously to compensate or avoid its
effects. He found the 'Sign of Liebreich' in only nineteen out of
sixty-two paintings; in a further twelve there were in fact no
shadows to depict (see Appendix 4).

Cataract
===

An acquired colour-blindness develops during the course of a number of eye disorders, generally those which have the effect of interposing a coloured filter between the retina and the outside world. Of these the most familiar is an opacity of the lens of the eye, known as a cataract.

In most elderly people, such opacities begin to form within the lens of the eye, and rarely provoke more than a little progressive blurring of vision. In addition to an overall mistiness, the advancing cataract absorbs principally the shorter spectral wave-lengths, starting with the violet and blue; and ultimately it may permit little beyond the red rays to reach the retina. Conversely, after the cataract has been extracted by an operation, the sudden influx of these excluded blue rays, in the presence of an established adaptation to a rosy world, may abruptly change the red vision into a temporary blue vision.★

This colour change is mainly apparent with the rather less frequent 'nuclear' type of cataract, which tends to become yellowish or even reddish-brown (Colour Plate VIII); and it is generally more striking when the patient is already myopic, so that the convex spectacle-lens (needed to replace the cataractous lens which has just been removed) is of comparable power to the concave (myopic) lens needed previously.

This was strikingly demonstrated by two paintings (Colour Plate XI) made by a myopic artist of the flowers in a vase beside his bed, a few days after his operation. At that stage the sight of both eyes was equally indistinct (without their respective spectacles), but he was overwhelmed at the contrast between the reddish colours from his unoperated (very myopic) eye and the bluish colours from the eye that had just been rendered hypermetropic by having its cataract removed.

★The author Charles Singer retained as exhibits both of the yellow-brown cataracts that he held responsible for this affronting change in colour.[20] An artist (H.S.) has recently reported that, as her cataracts advanced, she was increasingly puzzled by the pinks and reds in her garden, which seemed so much brighter than usual, and that she is now impressed by the vivid crimsons and vermilions of sunset. A Civil Servant (G.M.), recently relieved of a brown cataract, volunteered that everyone appeared to be wearing blue eye-shadow, their lips seemed rather purple, while a blueish haze covered all the buildings.

To most people who have their cataracts removed, the abrupt-
ness of this change is softened by the time-interval between the
two operations, and the latent period that must elapse before the
de-cataracted eye can resume clear sight through its new spectacles. But even artists whose professional life is so concerned with
colour may little realize how blue their world has then become.

A colour-change towards red can be noted in the later paintings
of many artists, and in a few of them it is tempting to attribute
this change to the progress of a senile cataract. A ready candidate
for this is Turner (Colour Plates IX–X), whose later pictures are
well known to have become more blurred and at the same time
increasingly suffused with red and orange light (in Mark Twain's
crude description, 'like a ginger cat having a fit in a bowl of
tomatoes'). The medical evidence of a cataract is indeed lacking,
but at least we know that Turner was not myopic, since his
reading glasses (of $+3.0$ D and $+4.0$ D) are preserved in the print
room of the Ashmolean Museum; it must be conceded that the
Mr Bartlett, who tended Turner in his last years, and who styled
himself 'surgeon-dentist and cupper', probably knew little (and
wisely said nothing) about his eyes. It could also be added that
when Turner was only twenty-three, his preference for reds and
browns was noted in Farington's diary, and, when aged thirty-
one, Sir George Beaumont had criticized his 'jaundiced tone'.[21]

At Turner's death in 1851 the only knowledge of his medical
history comes from William Kingsley's admission in a letter to
Ruskin that 'The simple truth is his digestion failed through loss
of teeth, and he had to have recourse to stimulants, and finally
took too much.'

It was Liebreich again who, in a paper to the Royal Institution
(in 1872),[22] first suggested that a lens 'sclerosis' was responsible
for this changing style of artists, and cited Turner and Mulready
as likely examples. In Turner's case he suggested that the distortion
which accompanied the blurring, along with the overall redden-
ing, were due to the secondary astigmatism that such a sclerosis
of the lens may induce. With respect to Mulready, he noted how
this change in colour value was particularly well shown in two
pictures in the Victoria and Albert Museum, one painted in 1836
and one in 1857 when the artist was seventy-two; both are of
essentially the same subject, but 'if we look at the second picture

through a yellow glass, the difference between the two almost
entirely disappears, as the glass corrects the faults of the picture'.
In Turner's paintings Liebreich noticed, after 1831, an increasing
'streakiness', the length of the streak being proportional to the
intensity of the light; and after a few years this diffusion of light
from the most intensely illuminated areas became increasingly
vertical. In Mulready's advanced age, he had been blamed for
painting 'too purple', with shadows in flesh as pure ultramarine;
all of which, said Liebreich, could be cleared by viewing them
through a filter, the colour of pale sherry.

This same observation was also made about Domenico Becca-
fumi's paintings, in which Guaita[23] found a constant deficiency
of violet; he reckoned that this artist saw colours as if through
a yellow glass, and the colours he used in daylight paintings
approached those we see in artificial light (presumably gas-light,
since he wrote in 1893). In the same year Angelucci added to
those whom Liebreich had quoted the name of Luca Signorelli,
whose later pictures are mostly in reddish-brown and orange-
yellow – often rather 'washed-out and wax-like' – a complete
change from his youthful palette. There are many other classical
artists whose names would be added to this questionable catalogue: Titian perhaps, or Guido Reni, or even Renoir (if one has
not already ascribed his reddish-oranges to his myopia); but this
attribution is at least plausible where there is later evidence of a
cataract operation.

Antonio Verrio is best known in England for his spirited mural
paintings during the late seventeenth century, culminating in the
allegorical picture of William III that crowns the Great Staircase
at Hampton Court. His earlier paintings are less familiar, but at
the age of only twenty-one he had painted a ceiling in Naples (subsequently destroyed), and in it he apparently included, with strange
prescience, a portrait of himself as a blind man led by a dog.

He continued painting in Hampton Court, working his way
down the garden front that had just been completed, and he
finished with the drawing-room of the new monarch, Queen
Anne. In describing this room, Edward Croft-Murray[24] disposes
briefly of Verrio's rather maladroit conception of Queen Anne
in glory (attended on the walls by her stumpy husband and an
appropriately dormant cupid), which was all in a surfeit of pink

Self-portrait of Antonio Verrio, c. 1700.

colours, and concludes: 'with its riot of ill-matched colours and unprepossessing faces and figures, it hardly stands as a brilliant finale to Verrio's career. Perhaps we may excuse him in part, for his sight was beginning to fail.' Soon afterwards his self-portrait, now in the National Portrait Gallery, London, was completed (possibly by a friend), with its pathetic inscription: 'Cieco Antonio il povero Verrio.' Two years later, in 1707, he was dead. Thirteen years after this, an advertisement was published by a Dr T. Clarke, stating that, 'to her late majesty Queen Anne's great satisfaction, Signor Verrio, the famous painter, was restored to perfect sight in Hampton Court, of a blindness called gutta serena'. The evidence all suggests that this was a cataract. The fact that Verrio never recovered his sight had been concealed by the unscrupulous oculist.

Another painter who developed a double cataract was Monet, and the characteristic changes are apparent in his latest paintings. Up till 1905 his whites and blues were still unalloyed, but soon after that the whites and even the greens became increasingly yellowish, and the blues more and more purple. He wrote in despair that 'Reds appeared muddy to me, pinks insipid, and the intermediate or lower tones escaped me ... What I painted was more and more dark, more like an "old picture" ... and when I compared it to my former works, I would be seized by a frantic rage, and slash all my canvasses with my penknife.'[25] He was reduced to labelling his tubes of paint and keeping a strict order on his palette, and to avoiding bright sunlight (which by constricting the pupil often further embarrasses those with central cataracts). In the final pictures, such as those of the water-garden at Giverny, which were done after 1920 when he had turned eighty, the form also becomes vaguer as his sight manifestly began to fail. He struggled on, aware that the artists Daumier and Mary Cassatt had both had cataract surgery without success, but in 1923 was persuaded by the Prime Minister, Clemenceau, to submit. After he had recovered from the operation (quoting Gillet) 'his first sensation was that of a diffuse blueness, and, having returned to his home, he was surprised at the strange colours of his most recent pictures.' So that it seemed he had been painting 'through an opaque glass'. The powerful lens ($+14$ DS $+7$ DC) permitted limited sight with distortion of shape as well as of colour, but he returned to work with enthusiasm, depicting 'violent landscapes, increasingly febrile and hallucinated, with impossible colours, all red or all blue'; and retouched his earlier paintings until all his friends and relations persuaded him to desist. Three years later he died. How interesting it would be to know whether he was 'touching out' the reds and oranges that might have insidiously been slipping in. One *Times*[26] critic has noted how some paintings 'just before his cataract operation were very unpleasant indeed, with their coarse handling of paint and bilious colouring'; whereas, after surgery, Sacha Guitry[27] has related how he found Monet in his studio, sitting alone before his palette, and groaning in deep distress, 'I can no longer see yellow'; and Monet finally gave up – saying, *'Le peintre opéré de la cataracte doit renoncer à peindre.'* Happily, with modern techniques this is now far from true.

Edward Ardizzone,[28] the distinguished contemporary artist, has described the result of his cataract extraction as follows: 'Through my operated eye I see a much colder, brighter world, in which reds become pink, greens greener, and blue more intense. At first the difference was startling.' For him the main difficulty was the change in scale: 'Everything looks bigger and closer; . . . and then the hardness and brightness: in looking, for instance, at a face, one sees too much. The down on a lip, every wrinkle and pimple, and the stubble of a beard. This wealth of detail makes it difficult to sort out the wood from the trees . . . I am rapidly getting used to the new vision and am unconsciously making all sorts of adjustments. All the same, when my second eye is operated on, I am going to miss the smaller, kinder and rather misty world I have loved so well.'

One must remember, of course, that this colour-change would only be expected in the rarer form of cataract, which becomes brownish as well as opaque – and of course it would apply only to naturalistic painters. Sir Matthew Smith, whose cataracts were removed shortly before his death, was unaware of any alteration in colour values; the only changes he conceded were that the colours had become brighter and the details clearer.

In assessing this theory – that the artist with a reddish cataract will paint increasingly in reddish colours – the first objection that usually springs to mind is that his reddened percept should correspond equally to a normally coloured world as to a normally coloured canvas, so that he might be expected to make the canvas emerge in the same colours as the original, however falsely he imagines both to be redder than they are. This self-regulating effect normally ensures that the subject and rendering do correspond in the case of astigmatism (hence the basic improbability of the theory about El Greco's elongations), but with the red cataract the problem is rather different.

I Degas, *Ballet Dancers*.

II Edward Gordon Craig, projected design for Act II of Ibsen's *The Vikings*, 1903.

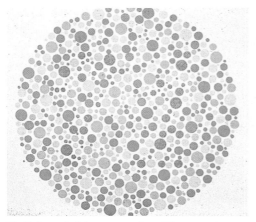

III Colour-deficiency test plate. The normal-sighted read the figures as 74, but the red-green blind read them as 21.

IV A copy of Van Eyck's *Mystical Lamb* by a colour-deficient patient exhibits the common inversion of red-orange and yellow-green, the blues being more or less correct (Lanthony).

V In a copy of Gauguin's *Ta Matete*, by a patient with dulled awareness of green, the colours of the dresses are shifted in the direction of green, yellow becoming greenish, red-orange becoming yellow (Lanthony).

VI Paul Henry, *Dawn, Killary Bay*. Henry was proven to be partially colour blind.

VII Painting by a colour-blind student.

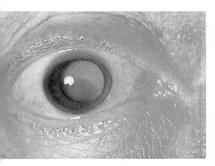

VIII The 'nuclear' type of cataract is often reddish in colour and thus acts as a reddish filter before the light.

IX Turner, *The Shipwreck*, 1805.

X Turner, *The Sun of Venice Going to Sea, c.* 1843.

XI Pre- and post-cataract surgery. Paintings by Sargie Mann.

XII-XV Louis Wain, paintings of cats made during a schizophrenic illness, 1926.

XVI Van Gogh, *Crows over the Cornfield*. Van Gogh's later paintings reflected the overwhelming depression of his final years.

If one wears a brown-tinted spectacle lens, this will cut out all the blue rays, so that blue objects seem dirty grey; greens (which are intermediate between blue and yellow) become yellower and purples (intermediate between blue and red) become redder. If one tries to paint with such spectacles, all the blue range of colours become less exactly differentiated and muddier. So the artist with a brown cataract who paints rosy scenes is rather in the position of the colour-blind who, as we noted, tend to keep clear of the colours that seem less distinct and less colourful. On the other hand, when such a cataractous painter feels compelled to use blue, he generally exalts it in order to reach through his lowered blue-perception (thus conforming to the minority reaction among the colour-blind).

In this way, perhaps, we can account for the single patch of blue that Turner usually interpolated right up to the end of his life, but as an almost isolated hue in strong contrast to the seemingly endless variety of reds, oranges and yellows which he was using in the same painting.

Or else it may be that the memory-picture has become so established that the artist-patient who experiences a relative blue-vision after losing his cataract, contrasts this with that rosy memory-picture of the world, which had become accepted as the true colouration. Even so, in spite of his distorted colour-sense an artist with such a cataract may well attain a more correct evaluation of the world by various secondary means. Thus he may have a long-established familiarity with his own pigments, so that, on seeing, for instance, a reddened tree, he mixes them in proportions that he knows from the past will give that very hue, even though the canvas as a result seems to him disproportionately red.

It must be admitted that age itself normally shifts our colour-values so that our view becomes yellower as we pass middle age. This can be confirmed by matching on a 'colour-rule', and attributed to a natural increase in the yellow pigment at the central spot of the retina (the 'macula lutea'), with the result that blue is increasingly absorbed and therefore less appreciated. As a consequence of this darkening of macular pigment, which should cause a relative blue-blindness comparable to that from a brown cataract, elderly painters might unconsciously seek to compensate by stressing their blues, or else to avoid the blue colours as they become less colourful and discriminable. Indeed this change might even be said to apply to Rouault, whose obituarist observed how 'claret-reds gave way to a profusion of yellow-greens'. After spending his life painting 'twilight', Rouault said: 'I ought to have the right now to paint dawn.'[29]

Other Secondary Colour Distortions

Alterations of our colour values can be caused by many disorders other than that provoked mechanically by the reddish-brown filter of a senile cataract or disturbances of the macular pigment. Indeed almost any debility can distort one's colour values. Thus William Wallace recorded, 'In dyspeptic states the colour vision is altered, and artists copying pictures while suffering from a bilious attack sometimes discover that, after recovery, what appeared to be a faithful copy is false and crude in colouring.'[30] The commonest change is a 'Xanthopsia' or yellow vision, which is a characteristic feature of poisoning by a wide miscellany of drugs, including santonin, digitalis, phenacetin, chromic and picric acids, and even snake venom; it is also occasionally noted in diabetic retinopathy and in glaucoma (even anticipating visible changes in the retina).

Indeed, 'seeing yellow' has been recorded since Roman times, when Lucretius,[31] Varro and Cassius described it simply as a stigma of the mentally unsound. To Galen it was due to 'hyposphagma' (blood in the aqueous humour); subsequently the yellow staining of the coats of the eyeball in jaundice suggested that bile was the cause of this curious symptom, a view that was believed (in spite of the fact that the cornea remains uncoloured in the deepest jaundice) by speculators even as late as Goethe. But the evidence for this view is still lacking in the occasional cases of xanthopsia that turn up; probably the Romans were right after all, and the yellow colour simply reflects a psychopathic quirk. The alterations of colour-vision in psychosis and drug-induced narcosis lend support to this;[32] a common description quoted from patients in ether abreaction was, 'Everything was yellow, bathed in glorious sunlight.'

Psychopathy can indeed provoke almost any colour disturbance: one patient has been reported[33] who had a specific inability to see red, simply because his wife had deserted him some years previously, wearing a bright red coat, and ever since he had managed to blot out this disturbing reminder of the traumatic incident.

Total colour-blindness is extremely rare – about one in 100,000,000 of the population, and may be the sequel to localized damage to the brain, as in the case of Jonathan I,[34] a professional artist of sixty-five who lost all his colour awareness after a car accident.*

His first weeks were gloom-laden with human flesh looking 'rat-coloured', and 'abhorrent grey' everywhere, so that food was barely eatable even when his eyes were closed. (Another patient with total colour-blindness from a tumour in the same area had complained that everyone looked 'dirty' – even new-fallen snow.) The only small consolation was an apparently enhanced sense of smell. His first attempts to paint, using colours from his palette that seemed 'totally right', produced a kaleidoscopic welter, that made sense only when seen in black and white. (This recalls the wartime use as bombardiers of those with gross colour deficiency, who had the ability to 'see through' camouflage, undistracted by their confusing colour configuration.) But increasingly he found satisfaction by painting in monochrome and even turning his hand to sculpture. At first these paintings, of labyrinthine complexity, were powerful and distraught, reflecting his anguish; then he gradually reverted to a representational style he had abandoned thirty years before, and the pictures became sensuous and full of vitality, but always in monochrome. His revulsion for colour and brightness persisted, so that he felt at home only in dusk or darkness, for in twilight his vision was splendidly enhanced, like lemurs and other big-eyed primates that only emerge at night.

*Extensive neurological investigations blamed this on an injury to the 'visual association cortex', where colour is interpreted in its perceptual qualities (it has already been coded by the retina, and then assessed in its physical components by another part of the brain).

Influence on Painting
of Natural Eye Pigment

It is sometimes suggested[35] that the warmth of colour which different painters use depends primarily on how fair or darkly pigmented they are, since in the former case, the greater amount of light that filters through the wall of the eyeball gives a colder tone to the retinal image, and vice versa. As a crude generalization, Nordic painters do indeed have colder colour-tones than Latins, and the latter than the central Africans or Polynesians; and, as if in confirmation, two recently tested albinos were both found to have defective colour-vision at the red end of the spectrum.[36] Conversely, some people carry more yellow pigment at their macula and might therefore be expected to be relatively insensitive to the blues and violets; and to this macular pigment has been attributed[37] the brighter, warmer centres in some of Corot's paintings, as well as the common artists' habit of heightening the blue of shadows in the periphery of outdoor scenes.

★

It should not need to be emphasized once again that all these theories which interpret the colouring that an artist uses, whether they relate to his personality, his inherited colouring or colour-blindness, or his acquired eye-disorders, can never be substantiated. Even if true, such factors are among the least important in determining the artist's style; and there are many other external influences (the availability of pigments, the instability of the green pigment used by most Renaissance artists, the environmental colouring of the artist's studio and so on) that we have not considered. All such mechanistic interpretations are rightly suspect, but not always wholly untrue.

CHAPTER FOUR

═══

RETINAL RIVALRY
AND UNBALANCED EYES

As the vertebrates evolved and their eyes moved round to the front of the head, their respective fields of vision began to overlap; thus an increasing area of the outside world, lying straight ahead, was registered by both retinas. Our more primitive terrestrial forebears – amphibia, reptiles and lower mammals – remained largely nocturnal or crepuscular; in the mud or undergrowth of their common habitat, with their activities dominated by touch and smell, they did little more than amalgamate this doubled image from the overlapping areas of their visual fields. But when primates and birds became treeborne or airborne, the wind blew all the smells away, and vision became the predominant sense; along with the development of colour discrimination, we learnt to utilize this overlapping field of vision to give us accurate judgement of distances, which became enhanced when a full stereoscopic view was achieved.

Thus, whereas most mammals can hold their eyes straight (i.e. with their visual axes parallel) when looking straight ahead, on looking to either side their eyes normally act independently, with widely divergent axes. Only with the higher primates does binocular vision become so important and so well-developed that we keep our eyes straight nearly all the time, by a complicated conditioned reflex which we learn during the first years of life in the interests of single three-dimensional vision. But if illness or anxiety hinders our adaptation during those difficult formative years, and particularly if the eyes have an inherited tendency to deviate, they may drift out of alignment, becoming convergent or divergent. Such a squint can equally develop later in life after an injury to the controlling eye-muscles or their respective nerves,

Correggio, a detail from Mercury instructing Cupid before Venus.
Venus is portrayed with a divergent squint.

and the deviation can be vertical as well as horizontal; while any
eyes that are poor-sighted will likewise have little incentive to
stay straight.

A squint is commonly thought to be unsightly, but in earlier
societies it has often indicated godliness and even beauty. Certain
early Caribs used to force the eyes of their children to squint by
severing the tendon of the rectus muscle through its overlying
conjunctiva. Venus herself was frequently described as having a
cast or squint, although the exact meaning of the word 'paeta' is
questioned.*

Minerva flavo lumina est: Venus paeto.
'Auctor Priapeorum' 37 (Aurelius Augustinius), AD 51. [Minerva has golden eyes, Venus a cast.]
Non haec res de Venere paeta strabam fecit?
'Priscianus' (M. Terentius Varro), c. AD 500.
[Did this not confer a squint on cast-eyed Venus?]
Si Paeta est, Veneri similis. 'Ars Amatoria' 2/659, Ovidius Naso, 45 BC–AD 17.
[If she has a cast, she is like Venus.]
  Unfortunately the iris, lips and hair of classical statues of this period were either insecurely
plugged in or only painted on, and where the plug fell out or the paint (and therewith the
expression) was destroyed by weathering, even the sex became doubtful.[1] By the time of the
Roman Emperors, when the pupils were properly chiselled in, the eyes are generally found to be
straight. Even so, the painting of Venus by Correggio in the National Gallery, London, has
frankly divergent eyes, and probably only a modest degree of squint was acceptable. To those
with a gross squint tradition has often conferred the gift of second sight or of casting the evil eye.

The Squint in Art

A squint is a common disorder; but such a deviation of the eyes should have little direct influence on an artist's style.

The most famous of all squinting painters was Guercino: this

'Il Guercino' *(the artist Giovanni Francesco Barbieri), painted by Benedetto Gennari, showing the gross convergent squint that provoked his nickname.*

was his nickname, and simply means 'the squinter'. His self-portrait makes no attempt to conceal that convergent and doubt-less poor-sighted eye, and his paintings may be said to have a rather two-dimensional quality, as he could have painted with only one eye (as did Sir Alfred Munnings, the PRA, who became blind in one eye at the age of twenty).

Dürer, Portrait of his Mother.
Her divergent squint was presumably passed on to her son.

Of more interest perhaps is Dürer, who had a divergent squint
(apparently inherited from his mother – *see above*). His various
self-portraits rather aptly illustrate the clinical sequence of this

Dürer, Self-portrait Aged Thirteen *(1484).*
The eyes are still straight.

type of squint, which (unlike the commoner 'cross-eye') usually
starts in older children, intermittently at first, and gradually
becomes less easy to control as the years pass. In Dürer's first self-

Dürer, Self-portrait Aged Twenty-two (1493).
His head is turned to the left, conceivably to compensate for the divergence
of the right eye.

portrait, at the age of thirteen, his eyes were straight, the right
eye then appears to have drifted outwards, which perhaps explains
the turn of his head to the left in the Louvre self-portrait (1493),

Dürer, Self-portrait Aged Twenty-one *(c. 1492).*
The right hand would seem to be warding off the confusing false image
from his divergent right eye.

seeking to lessen the deviation and therewith the tendency to see
double. A year previously the self-portrait from Erlangen
shows his right hand seemingly warding off any confusing
second image seen by his diverging right eye, and in that from
the Lehman collection in New York he seems to be holding up
his fingers to give a point of focus for the right eye and help it
to stay in alignment. In the later self-portraits the right divergence
has clearly become established; but in the last self-portrait, it is

Dürer, Self-portrait Aged Twenty-two *(1493).*
The fingers may have been held up in order to steady the right eye,
which is tending to diverge.

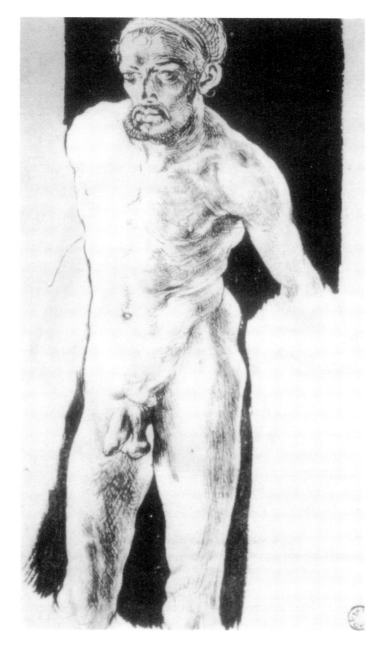

Dürer, Self-portrait in the Nude *(?1500–12).*

Dürer, Self-portrait as a Sick Man (c. 1510).
It is the left eye that now appears to be diverging, perhaps because the earlier self-portraits were done through mirrors and this was largely done by apprentices.

the left eye that seems to be diverging, perhaps because the drawing had been completed by an assistant, rather than by Dürer copying his own features in a mirror or, as can happen with engravings, because of a reversal of the plates. (In fact this picture was drawn simply to help his doctor in Paris to send back the

Thomas Inghirami, *showing a divergent squint in a painting by Raphael.*

most appropriate medicine, being inscribed: 'This is where the yellow spot is, and I am pointing to it with my finger: that is where it hurts.')

Various subjects of portraits as well as the artists themselves have had their squints immortalized. Thus a convergent squint has been noted in several portraits of Mozart.[2] Thomas Inghirami was painted by Raphael with his head turned slightly to the left and his eyes well over to the right (a compensating posture similar to that of the Dürer self-portrait in the Louvre): in his case the evident prominence of the right eye suggests that it was a very short-sighted eyeball, to which the squint would be a natural sequel. A similar divergence is apparent in the myopic, prominent and poor-sighted right eye in Degas' self-portrait.

Federigo da Montefeltro. *Painting by Piero della Francesca.*
Federigo's portraits were all done in profile to conceal the absent right eye.

This recalls the even more prominent eye of Federigo da Montefeltro, whose many portraits were all done in profile to conceal the still more unsightly socket of his other eye, which had been lost in jousting (he had the bridge of his nose gouged away, so as to give this remaining eye a better view on the blind side!); Cardinal Wolsey also permitted portraits only in profile

because of the blemish in his right eye.[3] So did the Duke of
Cumberland (Queen Victoria's 'wicked uncle'), whose left eye
had been destroyed in battle and who vainly trailed his whiskers
and moustache over the unsightly scars. (His brother, the admir-
able Duke of Sussex, who submitted to cataract surgery in the year
of Victoria's coronation, coped well thereafter with seventeen

El Greco, St Luke.
Divergence as the eyes as affectation of other-worldliness.

different pairs of spectacles.) Leon Gambetta, the flamboyant
President of France after Napoleon III's collapse, who escaped
from the Siege of Paris in a balloon, had a grossly distended right
eye (the sequel to a childhood injury); it was finally removed by
de Wecker, who himself signed the bottle in which it is still
preserved. Prof. Amalric was able to demonstrate the retained

fragment of steel (which would have precluded any recovery of vision) by X-ray photography of the eye within its sealed bottle.

Sometimes, however, the divergence is the result of the artist's affectation, rather than his realism, when it is used to express ecstasy (if the eyes converge for near vision, it would seem natural for them to diverge when looking to a far-off celestial world).

Aleijandinho, The Bad Thief. *His portrayals frequently had widely divergent eyes, emphasized by a broadening of the nasal bridge.*

Indeed, it became such a habit of El Greco's saints that their eyes even diverge when downturned, as in the paintings of St Simon and St Luke. The eighteenth-century Brazilian sculptor Aleija-dinho[4] also gave a gross divergent squint to most of the saints he depicted, often supplemented by a broadening of the nasal bridge (an occasional congenital anomaly, called 'hypertelorism'), which recalls the eye-disposition of most lower animals.

In fact most portrait-painters consciously or unconsciously give their subjects a slight degree of divergent squint to convey a more spiritual impression, as we can demonstrate by contrasting the relative positions of the reflected highlights on the two corneas.

An upward roll of the eyes is also used as an artistic affectation, when the painter seeks to give dramatic emphasis to the blindness

Peter Brueghel, Parable of the Blind.
Brueghel has been labelled the 'arch-diagnostician of eye ailments', because of his frequent illustration of the different types of blindness.

of his subject, whose eyes seem to turn desperately upwards searching for the sunlight, as in the familiar beggars of Brueghel,★ an affectation that is also adopted (for the same reason) by the hysterically blind.

Latent Squint

No eyes remain exactly parallel, when deprived of any incentive to fuse their two near-identical images – as in sleep or darkness.

★Peter Brueghel the Elder is said by I. M. Torrilhon[5] to have been the arch-diagnostician of eye-ailments, the five beggars from his parable of the blind representing, from left to right, ocular pemphigus with secondary corneal opacities, photophobia possibly from an active kerato-uveitis, phthisis bulbi and corneal leucomata. A similar painting by Hokusai has the blind men descending from right to left, possibly reflecting his racial directional gaze (see p. 123).

Thus we all have a small degree of a squint that is normally latent; very exceptionally the degree of latent squint is enough to cause fatigue in the effort to keep the eyes straight and justify correction with exercises, prismatic lenses or even surgery.

This may indeed have been the case with Samuel Pepys,[6] in so far as we can deduce this from the copious complaints in diaries which he kept up to the age of thirty-six. His failing sight obliged him at that age to discontinue writing, for he believed that, like his great contemporary Milton, he was destined to become blind. His visual troubles have often been analysed,[7] particularly in relation to the transient relief he gained by looking down tubes made of black paper (which had been designed to reduce illumination, and thus to enlarge the pupil in cataract patients); these relieved him of the problem of binocular vision. The general conclusion is that he probably had a marked latent convergence, aggravated by long-sightedness; and when his oculist, Mr Turlington, ultimately permitted him to wear the strong convex glasses he needed, Pepys was able to continue his duties and studies till he died at the age of seventy.

Eye Dominance

Although about one out of every twenty pre-school children squints (and one in two among mental-defectives), by adult life a true squint is rarely seen, and the eyes work in easy harmony. Nevertheless, even when both eyes have equal acuity of vision, one of them tends to have dominance over its fellow-eye, and to show this in various covert ways. Thus, if one suddenly points towards a distant object, by closing alternate eyes the pointing finger will be found to be more nearly in line with the master-eye than with its less dominant fellow. Such a preference for one eye, one arm or leg, and also for the directions in which we cast our gaze, can all have an influence on the personality, the writing and the artistry of the man. This 'laterality' is essentially a human attribute, and many have speculated on its origins and significance.

It seems that animals are nearly all ambidextrous, having no lateral preferences for hand or foot, unless this is dictated (as

Aristotle and Sir Thomas Browne observed) by a marked asymmetry – such as the lobster's claw. The left paw does seem to be preferred by cats, and a preference for the right paw by rats can evidently be annulled by cholinergic drugs or by excising part of the motor area of the opposite side of the brain; this is separate from any natural bias (found in cats, rats and dogs) to prefer a bowl of food placed on one or other side (this might depend on eye-dominance – which would indeed be difficult to test).[8] But apes show no lateral preference, nor indeed do most of the artefacts of Stone-Age man (except perhaps in some later flint chippings), nor indeed in most 'Stone-Age' tribes. Only with the Bronze Age is the right hand definitely preferred by Homer's heroes, and do right-handed sickles start to predominate, while the position of the animals in Bronze-Age cave paintings also suggests a left-to-right gaze preference. The first firm record is actually in the Book of Judges, where the tribe of Benjamin separated from its army all who were left-handed, and only 3 per cent owned up to it; for such a preference turns up in every primitive religion, and is often reinforced later, as in St Matthew's uncompromising Vision of Judgement, with the sheep on the right hand and the goats on the left.

So the roots of our own lateral preferences doubtless lie in that twilight world of totem and taboo, long before we started to become mainly right-handed, -eyed and -footed, when the right side became associated with sanctity, thence with the sun, strength and maleness, and the left with the moon and the reverse.

Indeed, this alleged 'femininity' of the left hand, reinforced by evidence from semantics and myth, has been held by some psychologists* to account for the occasional instance of artists like Paul Klee, who (quoting his son Felix) wrote naturally with his right hand, but preferred to draw or paint with his left hand; that is if we are prepared to count writing as a rational 'masculine' pursuit, and painting as intuitive and 'feminine'. Louis Wain,

---

*D. W. Winnicott[9] recounts a case of a headmistress whose divergent squint registered her split personality. Her left eye corresponded to her English-speaking father, an efficient, ordered personality, while her right eye registered her disorganized and religious, French-speaking mother. On her pro-paternal, well-organized days, she used her left hand and left eye, but retreated to her right hand and eye when she withdrew to the emotional world she shared with her volatile mother. With his full-blooded psychoanalytic approach, Winnicott also counted a convergent squint simply to be a reminder of the infant's early need and desire to focus on his mother's breast.

although normally right-handed, also depicted his cats only with his left hand; and a bizarre (if rather unconvincing) story is told how one day his right hand took over from the left and, instead of the cosy pets, depicted malign cats that became more and more fiendish, and ultimately fragmented as his madness deepened[10] (see Appendix 5 and Colour Plate XII).

So this right preference was probably imposed on our essentially ambidextrous human species by social and religious pressures rather than by any of the other fanciful alternatives that have been proposed – the overcrowding in the cranium, the directional circuit of the sun, the need to keep the left hand shielding the heart or (as Plato reckoned) the traditional stance of wet-nurses (Christian saints were often said to have proved their early sanctity by consistently refusing their mother's left breast).* In any event the mastery of the right eye and visual field probably soon followed.

Nowadays dominance of the left hand occurs in about 5 to 10 per cent of the population (estimates vary from 1 to 20 per cent), being almost twice as common in boys, and about twice as common again in imbeciles and schizophrenics – but not manic-depressives; it is also more often found in the first-born of ageing mothers, in breech deliveries and in those prone to epilepsy, migraine and immune diseases, as well as in artists, mathematicians and engineers. Famous 'sinistrals' include the prophet Ehud, the Judge of Israel (who turned his anomaly to such advantage), Jack the Ripper, Charlie Chaplin, George VI, Lewis Carroll, Paul McCartney and, among artists, Leonardo da Vinci, Holbein and Landseer.[12] Among Eastern races, left-hand dominance is probably more common among Semites and Hindus (there are no purely left-handed races), although statistics are scanty; and there has been an apparent increase recently among Western races, who no longer force their sinistral children to use their right hand for

---

*Aristotle tells us that the Pythagoreans described as 'good' anything which lay on the right-hand side. The left hand had apparently been ill-omened ever since the Earth Goddess persuaded her Titan sons to castrate their sleeping father, Uranus, handing a flint sickle to Cronus, who then grasped his father's testicles with his left hand and threw them together with the sickle into the sea by Cape Drepanum. In the Bible, honours, virtues and powers are constantly being awarded to the right hand, but not once to the left, and, in the Muslim world, the left hand has been further disparaged because it is traditionally used for toilet after defecation. In Albania sinistrals are still officially 'illegal'.[11]

writing, etc., as do the more traditional (and particularly Islamic) parents in the East.

Dominance of the right foot is generally associated with dominance of the right hand, and occurs in about the same proportion of the population. We normally step out with our right foot (as is said to be true of horses), in spite of the conventional drill instructions; and freemasons have used a left-foot launching as one of their cabbalistic signs, just as the Boy Scouts have adopted the left handshake.

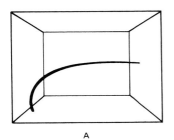 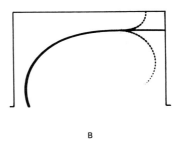

Directional gaze: *the glance-curve (after Gaffron) as seen (a) in perspective and (b) from above.*

An associated dominance of the right eye was first noted in 1883 by Lombroso, although about 30 per cent prefer using the left eye; and then all three were found to be related to a dominance of the opposite (left) side of the cerebrum, which, because of a crossing of the nerve fibres at the base of the brain, controls the right side of the body. There is, however, never a complete separation of left and right, and many intervening grades of ambidexterity exist.

We know that the left cerebral hemisphere also normally controls speech, while the right hemisphere contributes more to spatial recognition. Thus, blind children, although right-handed, usually 'read' Braille better with their left hands, since the message from their fingers may need interpretation by the right cerebrum, before being passed over to the left side for verbal coding.[13]

A further sequel to this hemi-cerebral dominance is the dominance of the field of vision that corresponds to the dominant eye, and therewith a greater ease in directional scanning towards that field. In other words, right-eye dominants find the right-hand side of the page easier to register, and their eyes sweep more easily towards that side than away from it.★

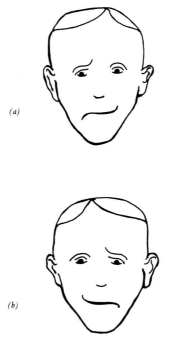

(a)

(b)

Directional gaze: *with these mirror images,*
(a) normally seems the happier, because our glance approaches it from the left.

The movements of our eyes in the horizontal plane are 'easier' than those in a vertical plane. This relates to our evolutionary past when our body axis lay parallel to the plane of progression, and the muscles of each side worked in unison with each other and in harmony with their fellows. (The lateralities did not really

★This dominance of the right field (to the right-handed) evidently depends on the underlying hemi-cerebral dominance and is not in fact a sequel to the directional scanning, since it is most evident with the use of identifiable symbols (and field dominance is least evident when we contrast 'nonsense shapes' or geometrical forms); and it is less selective in the left-handed.[14] Field dominance becomes less strong where the eye-dominance is greatest, suggesting that eye-dominance is a manifestation of highly differentiated functioning, and where this is well-developed, the subject can become relatively field-independent.[15]

emerge until we became erect, and the harmony, particularly of hand and eyes, was broken.) Since our gaze is thus naturally directed (in 'dextrals') into our right field of vision, our visual attention is indeed keenest in this right visual field, our natural tendency is to write from left to right while sinistrals tend to mirror-write from right to left.*

The natural sweep of the eyes in Western peoples does seem to follow a fixed path within the 'picture space' that is presented before us, our gaze being directed first to the left foreground, then penetrating towards the depth, and finally sweeping over towards the right (as in the upper diagrams on p. 119), and this regular pattern has been held largely responsible for the impression any picture makes. Any object lying within the compass of the path is 'recognized spontaneously', and those objects falling outside it (as in the right foreground or upper left background) must then be sought separately. The viewer of the picture tends subconsciously to locate himself at the beginning of this 'glance-curve' (i.e. in the left foreground), so that objects there appear as nearer and more important, even to the extent that the viewer will tend to identify himself with any character who is stationed there. Objects on the right appear, by contrast, less three-dimensional (more 'flattened out'), and instead of their texture, their colour and brightness seem enhanced. This pattern of localization, which Gaffron described (and which has been largely supported by later writers) evidently emerges most clearly in the right-handed and is absent in young children.[16]

It remains debatable to what extent this supports a structural basis of our aesthetic preference in pictures, but a recent survey[17] has shown that, for individual paintings, the influence of right-

*The first cuneiform writing was from left to right, if only to avoid smudging and concealment of the characters which had just been inscribed by the right hand which held the stylus. The primitive Sumerian cuneiform was then adapted to the Semitic languages of the invading Assyrians and Babylonians, and became (as Roman letters are today) the standard form for the whole civilized world, which included the Indo-European Hittites and Persians; and the Egyptians during the days of Akhnaton; it was resuscitated by the Seleucids after Alexander the Great, and continued for official documents right up to the time of Nero. Throughout these centuries writing flowed confidently from left to right, whereas the hieroglyphs of the early Hittites and Egyptians (which usually ran vertically) had no fixed direction. After the alphabet was invented, about 1500 BC, this was fixed by the Phoenicians to run, perversely, from right to left (one is tempted to suggest, at the whim of a defiant sinistral ruler). This the Greeks soon had the sense to rectify, to the perpetual advantage of all the European cultures that followed, while the Semitic languages were lumbered with their clumsy inverse script, counter to their natural scanning direction.

Velazquez, Jacob Receiving the Bloodstained Coat of Joseph, *and the left-right reversal of the same painting. To eyes that normally read from left to right the picture may seem less static in reversal.*

and left-handedness is considerable (as is also the sex of the observer), although, overall, the educational level of the observer is the more important factor.

Eye Dominance in Art

In Western countries, when our right eye is the master, and we read from left to right, our eyes are thus conditioned to sweep over to the right field whenever they strike the left side of the page (or canvas), and the gaze comes to rest on the right edge before undertaking another horizontal journey. Thus, according to one theory,[18] if we wish to convey a feeling of tension or movement (as in most baroque paintings), we place our principal subject to the left-hand side of the canvas; but if we place it to the right, the picture becomes calmer and more static. In Eastern races, who often write in the contrary direction, there may be a corresponding tendency to place the main subject-matter well over to the left (their pictures rarely seek any mood but serenity and calm). Indeed, P. Weinstein[19] independently observed that in Far Eastern paintings which are bisected obliquely from top-left to bottom-right corners the primary subject-matter is generally crowded into the lower left triangle, since gravity too plays a rôle, while the reverse is often true of Western art. It must also be conceded that the principal arbiter of the left-right judgement of paintings may well be just a question of familiarity; for when one group of students were shown[20] a series of paintings of various styles in alternate orientation, nearly all chose as correct whichever orientation had been first shown to them, and was therefore the more familiar; their agreement with the artist's intent appeared to be pure chance. Another batch of students were shown photographs, some of which had been reversed in the printing; 75 per cent guessed the correct orientation, but the reverse orientation was selected by those who were natural Hebrew readers.

The simple answer might be to record the directional gaze by cine-photographing an observer's eyes as he approached the painting, but this seems not to have been done. Incidentally, most Westerners, when asked to draw a face (or even a vehicle) will

Dürer, oblique shading in a right-handed artist.

point it to the left if they are right-handed; this is probably because they scan and write from the left, whereas most Arabs will point it to the right (whether right- or left-handed).[21]

Another influence of laterality on artists is apparent in the direction of their oblique shading, particularly in drawings and etchings. The natural oblique movement of the right hand is downwards and to the left, as we see in the drawing above, where the obliquity of Dürer's drawings is contrasted with that of Leonardo (see opposite) who, it seems, used his left hand not only in all his drawings, but even when he needed to avoid mirror-writing, and inscribe from left to right in order to be intelligible to others.[22]

Leonardo, oblique shading in a left-handed artist.

Yet a further influence of laterality is shown by the tendency of right-handed artists to bring in the light from the left side of the painting. Until the last century they usually had to paint in daylight, so they arranged the window on their left-hand side, with the model somewhat to the left of the painter, nearer the window, which thus illuminated the right side of the face. The model's right eye (the usual master-eye) looks directly at the artist, and the left eye is allowed the licence of a little divergence.[23] (Sometimes, as in Bronzino's *Portrait of a Young Man*, this licence is stretched to the limit.) This causes a curious contrast when the artist paints a self-portrait which, rendered through a mirror,

Bronzino, Portrait of a Young Man. *The model's right eye looks directly at the artist, and the left is allowed a little divergence — as is occasionally found in portraits by right-handed artists.*

causes the left eye to appear the master eye (and usually the right side of the face to be illuminated).

Aniseikonia

Very occasionally a rivalry between the retinas is brought out into the open, not as the sequel to a squint which frustrates their attempts to work in unison, nor by an uneasy dominance of the left cerebrum, but by a dissimilarity between the two retinal images, which cannot then readily be fused.

Such an 'aniseikonia' is almost inevitable when the two eyes have markedly different refractive errors; but this seldom matters, since one image is usually so much less clearly defined that it can be ignored whenever the discrepancy is great enough to confuse or blur the combined image. A. Linksz,[23] however, recently described an interesting experiment by an artist, Walter Humphrey, who, by wearing an aniseikonic lens, found that his paintings took on a distortion in the manner of El Greco and Cézanne, the faces becoming asymmetric and the contours drawn towards that side where the images were magnified. One must resist the temptation to impute this curious ocular anomaly to either of these masters, even when, as in the case of El Greco, the stretching of the contours is in a fairly constant direction.

Colour Discrepancies

Finally there are those who have different colour evaluations with each eye, not just as the natural (if usually unappreciated) sequel to a relative long- or short-sightedness on one side, but between otherwise identical eyes. Thus several artists find that they can see warm rosy tones with one eye, and cold blueish ones with the other; so they use one eye or the other, or both, according to the particular colour-value they are seeking. And in a recent press comment,[24] an East Anglian art-teacher affirmed that she 'sees independently with each eye, so that her eyes break down tones into pure colours'. The bizarre accomplishment admits no easy explanation.

This imbalance of colour awareness is, of course, unrelated to a difference of colour of the two eyes (or, more correctly, of the irises). Such a congenital 'heterochromia' (or, to Aristotle, 'heteroglaucos') often arouses comment, as with Alexander the Great, and with the soothsayer Thamyris, and the emperor Anastasios I (hence their nickname 'Dicorus'), and, in less worthy characters, the stigma of an Evil Eye.

CHAPTER FIVE

ENCROACHMENTS ON THE FIELD OF VISION

To our remotest invertebrate ancestors, vision was simply 'phototactic', deriving from scattered pigment spots that registered light and caused the animalcule to swim towards or away from that direction. As these pigment spots became organized into composite 'eyes', which gave a rough mosaic picture of the relative shapes of the objects that lay ahead, they served to identify food or give warning of attacking enemies. From that day on, the separable worlds of the hunter and hunted were born. For throughout the animal kingdom there is a division

THE OVERLAPPING FIELDS OF VISION

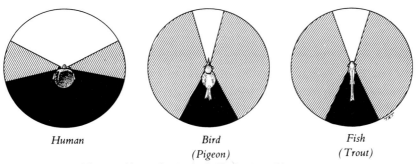

| Human | Bird (Pigeon) | Fish (Trout) |

The variable overlap in the field of vision of the two eyes.

into those who hunt their prey, who need not fear attack from behind and so can concentrate their visual powers on sharpening their acuity and distance-judgement at the expense of their visual fields, and the hunted, who have no need of sharpened sight for feeding (the grass they nibble or the plankton of the sea are there for the taking), but who need the widest possible field of vision to allow warning of the shadow of a predator approaching from behind.

The hunters, such as hawks and cats, bring their eyes round to the front of their heads, sacrificing their backward vision and concentrating their optic nerve fibres on a small central patch of the field, common to both eyes, with which they can distinguish the hunted mouse, in spite of his attempts at concealment. The 'hunted', on the other hand, keep their eyes well on the side of their head, and do not concentrate their acuity in the central point of their retinas, since attack may come from any angle; their aim is to have a fairly uniform vision over as much of the 360° field as possible, which will keep them informed of any movement in their wake that might bespeak danger, while they blamelessly graze away.

This dichotomy of hunters and hunted extends on through evolution into the souls of men, except that in the super-evolution of *homo sapiens*, where we no longer need to adapt our anatomy and physiology to our environment, but simply feed more into our cerebral computers, it is the insight rather than the sight that has become more canalized into the rapacious outlook of the human predator, or diffused into the perspective view of his humane but imposed-on fellow.

In mankind the fields of vision of the two eyes almost exactly overlap, and each covers an arc of about 180°, to include all objects that lie ahead, although the nose and eyebrows restrict the extent of these fields on the inner and upper sides. Many diseases encroach still further on this field of visual awareness, and may correspondingly intrude on the personality, and, in turn, on its artistic projection.

Glaucoma

In this major cause of blindness an impaired blood-supply to the nerve-fibres from the retina (aggravated by a raised pressure within the eye) gradually erodes the more peripheral parts of the visual field. Glaucoma is largely genetic in origin, and seems to have a preference for worrying businessmen and politicians (including two recent Prime Ministers). Creative artists are nearly always spared. James Joyce's glaucoma was purely secondary to his protracted iritis; and J. S. Bach's alleged glaucoma was almost certainly secondary to a thrombosis.[1]

Vitreous Opacities

The simplest intruders into the visual field are the little floating wisps, aptly named 'muscae volitantes' (= flitting flies), that most of us experience at some time, and which occasionally derive from a small haemorrhage into the vitreous chamber. Only rarely do these floating opacities become large or dominant enough to be a distraction. But to the introspective they can attain an even greater reality than the outside world; and such patients may come to feel that their personalities are, as it were, imprisoned, along with their unwelcome but ever-present 'floaters', within the confines of their own eyeball. Thus the Norwegian expressionist, Edvard Munch,[2] an introvert whose paintings reflected much of the alienation of his period, developed a 'haemorrhage' in the vitreous of his better eye at the age of sixty-seven, in 1930. The resulting opacity that cast its shadow on the retina was the more intrusive because his other eye was already poor-sighted; and the shape of a bird with a long beak began to insinuate itself into his paintings as the dominant subject of the world he depicted (p. 132).

Sir Joshua Reynolds, too, developed a vitreous haemorrhage in 1789, when he was sixty-five, and some months later, the other eye also weakened. The doctors called it 'gutta serena', which means little except that on casual inspection they could see no cataract lying white within the pupil. What he probably had was a retinal haemorrhage which then irrupted into the vitreous, since he had already suffered a paralytic stroke seven years earlier.

Two years later, as described by his contemporary biographer, J. Northcote,[3] he 'entertained strong apprehensions concerning the tumour which had been collecting for some time over his left eye' and had latterly been accompanied by much inflammation. The surgeons adopted every means (as they said) to 'discuss' it, but without effect; for it was afterwards discovered to consist merely of extravasated blood, and had no connection with the

Edvard Munch's late paintings show the intrusion of a bird-shaped vitreous opacity.

optic nerve. (They also submitted him to the usual regime of leeches, blisters and heroic doses of mercury, equally without benefit.) Following the advice of his 'most skilful practitioners', he abstained from painting women thereafter, hoping to save this remaining eye, 'a determination which cost him great pain'.[4] The following year he died, and an autopsy by the celebrated John Hunter revealed only a 'praeternatural enlargement of the liver along with a shrunken and flimsy right optic nerve'; the left eye is not mentioned. Conceivably a 'malignant melanoma' within the eye may have provoked the fatal damage to his liver, or perhaps Reynolds, like Turner, had succumbed to an alcoholic cirrhosis.

It would have been interesting (in our present context) if his later paintings had shown some characteristic form or colour change — perhaps the yellow-vision of a terminal jaundice from a cirrhotic liver, if not the red-vision resulting from a cataract or from an appropriately placed retinal haemorrhage* — but ever since his stroke he had put up his prices and farmed out more and more to his pupils, giving only an occasional touch of his own brush to justify the famous signature and the famous prices. According to Ellis Waterhouse,[5] his red pictures were sometimes attributed to Lawrence and the blue ones to Daniel Gardner, which would still further confuse any attempt at such an organic interpretation.

Phosphenes

Sometimes there intrude upon the visual field colours, lights and patterns, which are engendered within the retina itself, and are called 'phosphenes'. As children, we are often tantalized by the coloured panorama that is constantly provided for us whenever we shut our eyes, but as adults we tend to ignore this spectacle as our awareness becomes dulled. Only rarely do we manage to see them with the freshness of a child, even if we require a dose of

---

*The 'red-vision' resulting from retinal haemorrhage is not often noted, but one artist (N.T.) has recorded that since his macula was damaged by such haemorrhages, his paintings have all become deficient in blue (which he appreciates when this is pointed out to him).

LSD to achieve this, or re-learn the art, as artists do, of abstracting true colours from the toned-down and conventional colours we normally accept. Sometimes a little pressure on the eyeball helps to provoke such a coloured display. Thus William James[6] noted that 'beautiful patterns, which would do well for wall-papers, succeed each other when the eyeballs are long pressed', and Goethe recorded that he had a constantly recurring phantasm of a flower, whenever he closed his eyes and depressed his head, 'unfolding itself and developing from its interior new flowers, formed of coloured or sometimes green leaves, not natural, but of fantastic forms, and symmetrical as the rosettes of sculptors'.

These coloured 'phosphenes' are often provoked by children whose blindness from damaged eyes (retinal dystrophies, congenital cataract, etc.), as opposed to those whose blindness is due to an impediment in the brain and are 'blind to their blindness'. Such children have often been observed to poke their fingers into their orbits, so as to provide a psychedelic substitute for the natural vision from which they are debarred.[7]

Similar bright patterns can be induced by low-grade electrical stimulation of the intact brain, and these have recently been found to show a striking resemblance to the scribblings of young children. Still more significantly, they recall certain neolithic rock drawings, and even hieroglyphic forms. From some 300,000 drawings which pre-school children (of English, American, French, Chinese and Negro origin) start making about the age of three, Rhoda Kellog[8] identified twenty 'basic scribbles' and six geometrical diagrams, from which the combines and aggregates are constructed that finally lead to the pictorial representation. Out of these, the 'visual alphabet' seems to be formed (p. 135), which (as opposed to 'language alphabets') is probably common to all humans, regardless of race and culture.

Of a different quality are the little darting specks of light which we sometimes notice ('seeing stars') after a knock on the head or on suddenly standing up (and thus draining blood from our retinal vessels), and which are attributed uncertainly to shadows of the circulating retinal blood corpuscles. To the romantic mind these dancing lights can be decked with angelic vestments or metaphysical meaning. Thus, to the rationalist, the sparkling saints that Joan of Arc saw may have just reflected the lowered

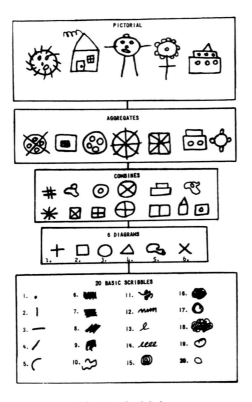

The Visual Alphabet.

pressure in her retinal vessels due to vicarious menstruation, since they appeared at monthly intervals, and her warders noted that she had no normal menstrual flow.

Macular Dystrophy

The commonest cause of registrable blindness or partial sight in Western countries is a degenerative change in the most sensitive, central patch of the retina (the 'macula'), usually just as a sequel to old age. This dulls and distorts, and finally blots out the details of the object to which the eye is directed, leaving the rest of the field of vision unblemished.

Right   Left

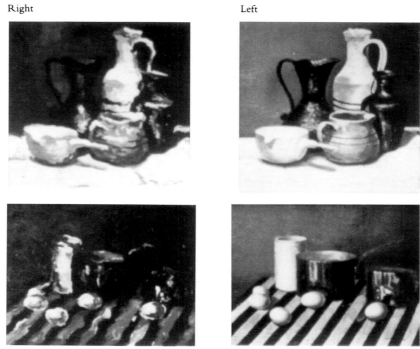

Macular dystrophy: an artist's experience (*Sperduto*[9]).
The right-handed picture of each pair is the view seen by the worse-affected right eye.

Most very old artists probably experience a little of this impairment, which may join the other impediments of an advancing
age − presbyopia, early cataract and so on, to augment their
increasing breadth of style, and so arouse little comment. Often
one eye is affected much more than its fellow, and occasionally
an artist will be confused by finding that the worse eye yields
darker paintings, with their loss of detail and distorted contours,
when contrasted with those from its less affected fellow.[9]

Damage to
the Visual Pathways
==

Other disorders that encroach on the field of vision derive from
progressive damage to the retina, as in retinal detachment, or to

the optic nerves as they pass back to imprint the retinal image onto the cerebrum. In the first category falls James Thurber, a high myope, who lost the sight of both eyes from retinal detachments in middle life. As his remaining eye failed, he struggled bravely to continue drawing his cartoons by using black crayons on huge sheets of yellow paper. When his 'fog' became too thick, he stopped sketching and learned to write by dictation, and his delightful fairy tale, *The Thirteen Clocks*, has all the distilled imagery and spontaneity of his earlier drawings.[10]

Many have speculated about the cause of Milton's blindness. In a letter to his friend, Leonard Phileras, Milton himself attributed it to 'cataract or amaurosis', since his eyes were not injured 'to outward view'. He even incorporated a play on the Latin name for cataract ('suffusio') and for amaurosis ('gutta serena') in one of his autobiographical echoes in *Paradise Lost*.★ Subsequent writers have suggested that his loss of sight was caused by progressive myopia.† Others have diagnosed albinism (in the egregious company of Tamerlane, Edward the Confessor and Noah), and the universal scapegoat – syphilis (in his case, it was allowed to be congenital). More fanciful diagnoses, very prevalent at the time, attributed his blindness to his political improprieties, and some even averred that it was a drop of the martyred king's blood that 'had quenched his eyes'.[11] However, from Milton's description in a letter of a darkness descending over 'the left part of the left eye', followed by a general restriction of his peripheral vision, retinal detachment and glaucoma were, until recently, considered to be more likely diagnoses.[12] The latest theory is that he had a pituitary tumour,[13] which could also account for some of the changes in his general health and bearing

---

★Thee I revisit safe;
And feel thy sov'reign vital lamp; but thou
Revisit'st not these eyes, that roll in vain
To find thy piercing ray, and find no dawn;
So thick a drop serene hath quench'd their orbs,
Or dim suffusion veil'd.

Paradise Lost, III

†Milton's father presumably was myopic, since (as Aubrey describes) he could read without glasses at eighty-four. His mother took to glasses at thirty; they were probably myopic, since astigmatic glasses were not available, and she is unlikely to have been so hypermetropic that she needed them so early in life.

during the years when his sight was failing, and when the charm and dignity of his earlier works was often replaced (as Mark Pattison put it) by 'the language of the gutter and the fishmarket'.

By 1652, when Milton was still only forty-four and had twenty-two years more to live, the light had failed completely and his mental stability returned. He wrote the sonnet on his blindness (*When I consider how my light is spent/Ere half my days, in this dark world and wide, ... They also serve, who only stand and wait*); and indeed, the reflection of his blindness keeps recurring in the great poems of his later years – *Eyeless in Gaza, at the mill with slaves* in Samson Agonistes; *But cloud instead, and ever-during dark/Surrounds me* in Paradise Lost. The serenity of his last decades contrasts with the roughness of his middle years. His domestic and political struggles had receded, and a contentment and resignation, that are often encountered in the totally blind, sustained him until his death.

One cannot help marvelling that the whole of *Paradise Lost*, in all its polysyllabic splendour, was written after Milton had lost all useful vision. It seems that he managed to dictate it all in snatches, often of a dozen or so lines, which he usually worked out during his many sleepless nights (wakening his daughter Anna with each inspiration, so that she could commit them to paper). All those harmonies, stresses, caesuras, crowded syllables and pauses that lend the poem its peculiar majesty come from the isolation – perhaps liberation – of his spirit during those early years of total blindness.

Wyndham Lewis, artist, novelist and critic, began to lose the outer fields of vision of each eye just before the Second World War. He was told by his London oculist that he (like Milton) had a pituitary tumour, pressing on the optic nerves, which should be removed. Unhappily the war drove him from England, and his apprehension (but not his sight) was relieved by vitamin injections elsewhere. On his return after the war, the tumour was inevitably much larger, and he was just able to complete the painting of T. S. Eliot in Magdalene, Cambridge, by sitting about six inches away from the canvas, before (as he affectingly described it in the *Listener*),[14] the 'sea-mist' that had been closing in from both sides, reached across the island of sight that remained, and

Wyndham Lewis, Combat Number Three, *1914*.

his days of painting were done.* At his autopsy only a parcel of nerve-fibres were found to be still surviving the spread of his fatal tumour (which can still be inspected in the pathological museum at Westminster Medical School).

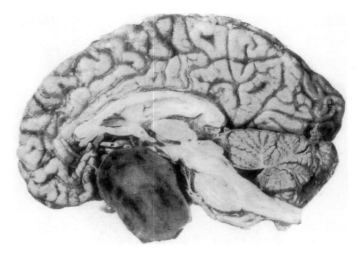

The brain of Wyndham Lewis.

Damage to the fields of vision from pressure still further back along the optic pathways causes a loss of field in both eyes, not of their outer fields, as with the pituitary tumour, but of the corresponding left or right sides in both (depending on which side of the cerebrum is damaged). This is a common sequel to cerebral thrombosis in the elderly, and such patients, being usually unaware of their blindness, may subconsciously fill in the missing half-field with a picture, such as would seem a natural continuation of the other half-field (on the unaffected side) which is seen normally. In the well-ordered psyche, such a covering-over of the defect may give a welcome feeling of security; although this may be rudely interrupted by meeting unanticipated obstacles on the blind side or when reading into the blind area is found to

---

*There is always a temptation to overstretch one's medical analogies to seek points in common between the work of two sufferers of an identical disorder, and then attribute this common feature to the malady in question. But Wyndham Lewis, with his brilliantly coloured paintings and his vorticist prose, could hardly be more alien from Milton's colour-images that were so sparse and sombre, and the 'organ-voiced' grandeur of his epic style.

be as frustrating as trying to read pages in a dream. To the unquiet mind, however, this empty canvas is asking for trouble, and into it can be deposited all the embarrassing memories and guilty desires that the ego has been trying to obliterate. Savin[15] has

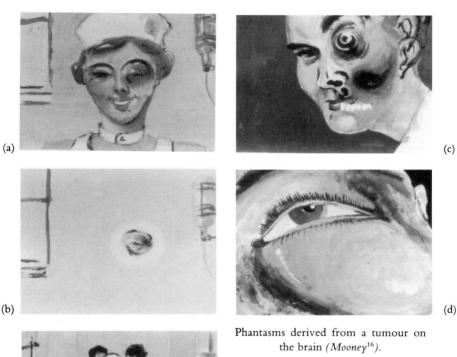

(a)

(b)

(c)

(d)

(e)

Phantasms derived from a tumour on the brain *(Mooney[16])*.

The patient, a commercial artist with disturbed sight from a 'parasagittal meningiome', tried to depict his nurse, and her left eye became; livid (a), persisting (like the smile of the Cheshire cat) after she had left the ward (b). The doctor's eye too became hideously inflamed (c), and then zoomed towards him when he closed his own eyes (d). Even when all seemed normal in the ward, little homunculi were liable to intrude (e).

described how the blind half-field in such a 'homonymous hemi-anopia' may become colonized by imagined strangers from whom there is no escape; or by freakish little intruders, whose lewd gestures, even backed by flashing purple lights and Wagnerian music, may plague the aged arteriosclerotic, especially if his conscience is unclear. And fanciful interpreters attribute the malign figures of Brueghel and Bosch to some such mishap.*

It has even been suggested that the scintillating haloes borne by so many medieval saints, and even the steps of Jacob's ladder, were simply projections of the auras of an attack of migraine (which is known to stem from a similar restriction of the blood-supply to the brain). In the case of St Hildegard there could be

St Hildegard seeing visions.

*The fully-sighted are normally spared these intrusions, at least when the eyes are open; but one author (A.W.) has described how, for over two years, he was constantly being disturbed by the portrait of his mother, who had died in his childhood, appearing whenever he closed his eyes; and another (P.W.) was beset by bizarre little figures that made him dread the time for sleep. In Germany this apparently clear vision through closed eyes has been labelled the 'Tiberius phenomenon'. It was noted in patients whose eyes were bandaged, or even removed; and some even claimed clear 'visual' images through the back of their heads.

Adjacent to this 'occipital' area of the brain, on which the visual images are reproduced, and then 'perceived' by the mind, lies a 'parietal' area in which such percepts are coordinated and rationalized; and several patients have been reported in whom injuries or tumours of this area may so upset the visual feedback that they can only draw or paint while both eyes are kept closed.[17]

some truth in this, since she describes in detail how the visions, which she painted so vividly afterwards, were preceded by waving lights or flames, often with definite 'fortification figures' and radiating from a coloured area (as do the classical 'scintillating scotomas' of migraine). And her descriptions should certainly not be dismissed lightly, since Hildegard was not just an ecstatic abbess, but a writer with an analytical approach unique in her period, for she was born in AD 1098, when the 'science' of the dark ages had barely emerged into the Arabian twilight.[18]

Damage to the nerve-fibres that pass backwards from the eye can also be caused by transient inflammations (such as an 'optic neuritis' from multiple sclerosis) or insidiously by poisons. The patterns of erosion and recovery of the visual field during a bout of 'retro-bulbar neuritis' have been nicely depicted by an artist in a series of paintings which he bequeathed to Moorfields Eye Hospital.[19] Whereas poisons such as tobacco may have a selective effect on our colour responses, causing a patch in the field of vision with diminished awareness of red and green. Thus of Maurice Greiffenhagen (RA, 1862–1931) it was said that his later paintings bear testimony to an excessive fondness for tobacco which had caused such a central 'colour scotoma'.

Psychedelic Art

The impact of other poisons falls on our visual nerve-fibres almost at the end of their long journey from the retina to the point in the brain where a conscious visual 'percept' emerges. LSD and other hallucinogenic drugs seem to cause an interruption of the 'association fibres' in the posterior lobe of the brain, which mould the unconscious cerebral image of the seen world into the conscious percept, altering it, in the light of our experience and needs, so that it falls into line with our established schemas, with all the attributes that we think proper for the object which we now can recognize. LSD thus allows us to see a far truer image than the ordered stereotype that our association fibres normally permit us to apprehend. It lets us see the true shadow-colours – the blue shadow in the snow, the green beneath the red object and so on, that we normally discountenance; for we can cope with the flux of our complex external world only if objects remain what we expect them to be, if snow is always white and houses are always vertical, irrespective of the tilt of the eye and the slope of the retinal image. To some extent these drugs restore to us the vision of the child, who makes no distinction between reality and appearance, and who can happily use an upturned table for a space-ship, a pudding basin for a helmet and so on.

The effect of hallucinogens on vision seems usually to fall into three phases, although such purely subjective experiences necessarily vary with the individual, the dose and the environment. The first, and the most enjoyable, is an escape from the dulling effect of familiarity, which allows a gradual heightening of the colours around us and an emergence of the shadow-colours, which we normally suppress and ignore. Together with this comes an increased awareness of the third dimension; for, again, we have become accustomed to ignore the blurring of distant objects when we focus for near, and vice versa; hallucinogenic drugs permit no such deceptive covering up of our limited depth of focus, any more than they permit one to smudge over the true colours we see. And so objects seem to attain a 'solidity' that enhances their quality and interest.

Aldous Huxley, who had become nearly blind in adolescence from a keratitis, moved to California during the war, trusting to be cured by some bogus eye exercises. When the blindness worsened, he wrote compellingly about the fascination of those hallucinatory drugs, which soon became embarrassingly popular.[20] He recalled how, in this first stage of intoxication,

... the perspective looked rather odd and the walls of the room no longer seemed to meet at right-angles. But these were not the really important facts. The really important facts were that spatial relationships had ceased to matter very much and that my mind was perceiving the world in terms of other than spatial categories ... What I noticed, what impressed itself upon my mind, was the fact that all [the books] glowed with living light and that in some the glory was more manifest than in others.

The awareness or the rediscovery of the beauty in those parts of the visual scene which had previously been taken for granted, or whose less strident colours had been overlooked or even frankly suppressed, is again recalled by Huxley:

A moment later a clump of red hot pokers, in full bloom, had exploded into my field of vision. So passionately alive that they seemed to be standing on the very brink of utterance, the flowers strained upwards into the blue. Like the chair under the table, they protested too much. I looked down at the leaves and discovered a cavernous intricacy of the most delicate green lights and shadows, pulsing with indecipherable mystery.

> Roses:
> The flowers are easy to paint,
> The leaves difficult.

Shiki's Haiku expresses, by indirection, exactly what I then felt – the excessive, the too obvious glory of the flowers, as contrasted with the subtler miracle of their foliage.

It may be an hour later before the second stage of intoxication becomes prominent, and it signals the increasing suppression of those other associations that relate us to the external world. We begin to mistrust the interpretations we make of all the images we are seeing. We no longer compensate for the shifting positions of the retinal image as we rotate our eyes, and thus the objects around us seem to jump about, in time with the movements of the retinal image; hence the jazzy and repetitive quality of some of the paintings executed under the influence of mescaline. And again, since the room we see is no longer our familiar room, with every object safely identifiable from its past associations, but a series of colours and patterns and contours, these assume far more relevance than the mere function and history of the objects to which these shapes and colours relate.

The excitement of this visual experience had indeed been vividly described by Havelock Ellis at the end of the last century:[21] 'how an ever-changing field of golden jewels, studded with red and green stones would spring up into flower-like shapes beneath my gaze, and then seem to turn into gorgeous butterfly forms or endless folds of glistening, iridescent fibrous wings of wonderful insects'.

The final phase follows when the progressive dulling of the associations that bind us to our sensory environment renders that environment less and less real. Fear mounts as the schizophrenia deepens; then, as the toxic effects of the drug begin to wane, a new security seems to return, and we gradually resume our earthly mantle; but the heady memories of our immortality remain, for we have seen the true colours, the true contours and the true perspectives, which with a conscious effort we can recall and enjoy for the rest of time.

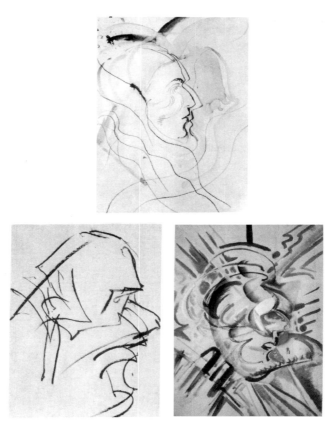

L. Matéfy, drawings made under the influence of LSD 25.

These truths that underlie our seen world, and which we habitually ignore, are indeed the stock-in-trade of so many great painters, who have not needed a hallucinogen to disclose what is there for anyone with perspicacity to apprehend. The brilliant and contrasting shadow-colours have been deployed by Impressionists and Post-Impressionists for nearly a century. The heightened sense of perspective that gives a three-dimensional quality to the central subject has been utilized at any rate since Renaissance

painters like Bronzino. The emphasis of contours and structural
content recalls particularly some contemporary paintings, such as
those of Merlyn Evans. The jazzy repetitions and the whirling
movements of the images recall the vorticism of Wyndham
Lewis. And the whole gamut of visual novelties has been popu-
larized in the recent vogue for psychedelic art.

Schizophrenic Art

There are certain parallels between the visual world and artistry
of the natural schizophrenic and those of the schizoid state induced
by hallucinogens. The 'perseveration' or repetitions of a sharp
visual image, so that it spills on to the succeeding images or
'jazzes' its way across the scene as the eyes rotate – a characteristic
hallucination after taking LSD (which is simply caused by a
heightened and prolonged formation of our normal 'after-
images') – is echoed in the fragmentations and in the reduplication
of the figures in many schizophrenic paintings.

Some schizophrenic artists achieve a bizarre and dream-like
quality that is the envy of many surrealists. Others, with visual
and verbal imagery overlapping, interpolate words or phrases
into their paintings, which again have the dream-like quality of
being slightly off-true, or even become fabricated neologisms.
And others, concentrating on elaboration and stylization, lose the
representation in a mosaic of colours, just as the conventional
cats that Louis Wain depicted often seemed to have fallen
apart into strange and horrific patterns, finally disintegrating into
a kaleidoscopic mass – traditionally thought to have formed a
chronological series that reflected the stages in his mounting
emotional tension (although their exact timing and order is now
questioned)[22] (Colour Plates XII–XV).

Indeed for many schizophrenics, painting has served as a safety-
valve, with which to externalize their confusion or despair; and
in many cases the exotic or compulsive renderings when they
were distraught are far more 'artistic' than the tame products of
their more balanced years. Thus, in the case of one artist who
was recently subjected to a frontal leucotomy, her timid post-

operation renderings are a pale echo of the fever and brilliance of those from a less contented past.

But in the case of those whose dementia permits little release of emotion, and who withdraw from the outer world, their paintings provide a clinical rather than an aesthetic interest. Their strokes may become tinier and tinier, till their contact with reality suffices only to let them make a few dots on the paper. Occasionally this shrinkage of the point of contact means that their whole world is shrinking; indeed, on occasion, it is they themselves who seem to be shrinking, as in Alice's Wonderland. One such patient described how his sudden self-shrinkings could only be stemmed by grasping objects that would relate his dimensions to the outside world. Again the depression of such schizophrenics often shows itself by a curtailment of the scene they are depicting to a series of basic forms that simply express their negativism and apathy, such as a hard empty horizon or the blank implacable zigzag of a mountain-range (cf. Colour Plate XIII).[23]

In general, the preferences of schizophrenics are for tactile rather than visual sensations (which is also found to be true in 'only' children).[24] Visual hallucinations are rare, by comparison with auditory and tactile ones, because vision is essentially a distance-sense and readily abstracted, while the near-senses, of touch and hearing, that entail 'involvement', become disturbed when their contact with the external world is lost.

Gross Loss of Visual Field – Near-Blind Art

When the loss of visual field is so extensive that only an occasional island of sight remains, drawing or painting may still be possible, in that the pencil can be seen to contact the paper; but these hardly count as visual arts, since the whole conception is essentially one of feeling rather than sight. Such near-blind artists, being released from the constraints of direct representation, are thrust into that haptic or kinaesthetic world that opens up a whole new system of values and a whole new pattern of imagery.

In his school of blind and near-blind children in Philadelphia,

Victor Lowenfeld[25] encouraged his pupils to make capital out of their limitations, and a remarkable series of drawings emerged. These emphasize the individual shapes that are interesting to the children – symbolically, haptically (for the quality of their texture and contours) and kinaesthetically (for their movement potential).

The three illustrations below were the successive drawings of a boy whose congenital cataracts permitted him to see only an area of about two and a half inches in diameter on his drawing-board. He had no knowledge of the overall contours of the head that he was depicting, and in this way he was like the blind sculptor who envisages a head as the sum of a multitude of small areas which he can map out with his fingers.

(a)   (b)   (c)

Paintings of a congenitally near-blind boy: stages in development (Lowenfeld[24]).

The particular interest of these three drawings is that they clearly illustrate the three stages of development that Lowenfeld described for all who are primarily subjective or 'autoplastic' interpreters, and who are spared from having their natural haptic evaluations overlaid by the influence of good vision. The earliest stage (a) is the diffuse representation of the whole image – apparently naturalistic because of its undifferentiated character: this he described as the 'stage of self-confrontation'. Then, after a while, comes a gradual appreciation of the separate elements of form and expression. 'This second stage (b) of development at some point becomes such an overwhelming discovery that it overpowers his whole concept; instead of our first, vaguely formulated, projection, we now have a structural overemphasis of the meaningful parts. The second stage then appears of almost geometric character, since the structural element has become vitally significant in the discovery and formulation of the self.' Only when the child has experienced the intellectual and emotional power to express his imagery, does he move on to the third stage (c) in which, as we see, the rigid structural and symbolic formulation gives way to a more flexible expression of his visual and haptic experiences.

A FURTHER NOTE ON MIGRAINE (pp. 142–3)
Giorgio de Chirico, into whose 'metaphysical paintings' zigzag patterns and jagged black figures were wont to intrude, suffered episodes of intense headache, motion sickness and even vomiting, which were labelled as migraines even by his contemporaries. (Ref. G.N. Fuller and M.V. Gale (1988). 'Migraine aura as artistic inspiration', *British Medical Journal*, 297, pp.1670–2.)

CHAPTER SIX

═══

TOTAL BLINDNESS

In our attempt to trace the influence on the personality of altered vision, we have considered in turn the optical, physiological and physical impediments that may curtail or distort the image that the brain receives. In all of these the blunting of sight is limited and, for those affected, the environment remains essentially that of a normal-sighted person, so that their terms of reference and emotional needs are conceived in our own familiar setting.

But when we consider those who are wholly blind, we enter a different country. Here the whole outlook is dominated by the absence of sight. The blind are set apart from the sighted, not just by the physical limitations and complete shift of sensory assessments, but because sight has become intimately associated with all our spiritual and sexual needs; and from this derives all the mythology and folklore that starts with the sun-gods, spreads through the concepts of second-sight, the evil-eye and so on, to be crystallized in the writings of Freud and his followers.

We must begin, therefore, by glancing through the earliest history of man, in order to comprehend the sources of these associations that are so fundamental in our attitude towards blindness; then we can rejoin the mainstream of our thesis in discussing the personal and social problems of being blind, their outward expression in blind art and literature, and finally the problems and adjustments that face those who have been blind and whose sight has been restored.

'In the beginning,' said the Hebrews, 'God made Light.' In the beginning, said the Japanese, God gave birth to the Sun-Goddess (who, in turn, begat Japan and its race of God-emperors) while he was washing out his eyes. In the beginning, said the Egyptians, the proto-god Ptah fathered all the other gods through his eyes (and then the humans through his mouth).[1] And so, with endless variations, the story is repeated elsewhere. For to primitive man, worship of the sun must have been almost instinctive when he embarked on his first brave moments of conceptual thinking, along with an awareness of his existence and his destiny, and the hope or presumption that this was guided by some external force. The Sun-god, as the primordial giver of life, and as the source of the heat and light that sustained the life he had created, has remained supreme in almost every nascent civilization; and in some cultures he has never been replaced. To the more sophisticated classical world, the supreme deity tended to delegate his control of the sun to one of his favourite offspring – such as Phoebus Apollo or Horus – but the sun nevertheless remained the emblem of supremacy, and godliness was equated with light and evil with darkness, long before it was crystallized thus by the endless imagery of the Christian myth.

The human eye, as the receiver of light, the avenue through which the Sun-god's emanations reached us, thus became the symbol of the way to God for the *Vedas*, just as it was the symbol of Horus to the Egyptians. According to Euclid and Ptolemy antenna-like 'rays' travelled in the reverse direction – outwards from the eye – but the eye still remained the avenue of contact. By the Renaissance, the correct view (the older Epicurean 'Intromission' theory) was winning; and Leonardo accepted the theory that rays went outwards only 'when considering the beguiling power of a maiden's eye'.[2] Even so, extromission has continued as the basis of the belief in the Evil Eye right up to the present; and as recently as 1921 a reputable London doctor described in the *Lancet* 'an instrument set in motion by vision'.[3]

To the more mechanistically minded, the eye was also the passage of entry and exit for the soul, which was consequently held to reside where the optic nerves made union – at the pituitary body – or (as Descartes had it) an inch or two further back, in the pineal gland. This is our own vestigial third eye, and still functions as a third eye among certain reptiles; in mammals its functions are obscure, but it does contain a chemical that helps the cerebral function and which is specifically disrupted by LSD. The pineal body's function can be affected by changing light

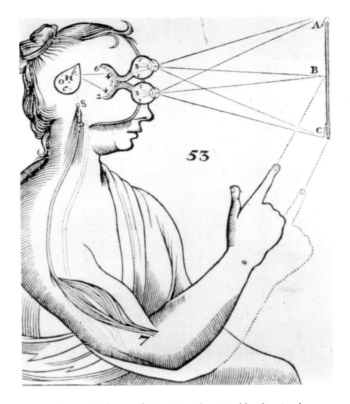

Descartes' theory of perception, dominated by the pineal.

conditions and it has been suggested that the religious festivals of the ancients, grouped around equinoxes and solstices, were thus arranged when stimulation of this 'third eye' made ecstatic experiences more accessible.

The association of sex with almost every form of religion is a commonplace, and the association of the sight with sex is a natural sequel; for where Godly light can enter, so can Satanic darkness, and the eye that looks wistfully to God at times looks libidinously elsewhere. Thus the eye can readily become (as Freudians have emphasized) the organ of projection or displacement from the genitals, whenever fear, guilt, inertia, impotence or despair barred a normal sexual outlet (see Appendix 6).

The seeing of sexual acts or images then becomes almost as exciting, or as guiltful (according to one's taste and inhibitions), as actually participating; and the group who find it exciting tend to become voyeurs, or, if of passive temperament, exhibitionists, just as those who are guiltful tend to become scotophiliacs. In our own less God-fearing days, it is the human neighbour more often than the divine father who looks into our guiltful eyes and discerns the source of our sexual shame. Hence derives the widespread use of dark glasses; for, although a small minority of those who wear them have an honest photophobia from albinism or inflamed eyes (or just wish to pretend that they are not myopic), a much larger proportion conceal their healthy eyes behind darkened glasses simply to screen their guilt from the penetrating looks of their fellows. Thus J. M. Heaton has described[4] one psychopath who travelled for her analysis only at dusk with veil, goggles and heavy-brimmed hat, and others who identified the sun and its light with their fellows' watchful eyes, detecting their incestuous desires.

The common practice nowadays of wearing ordinary spectacles that correct a trifling refractive error (which was not, itself, causing symptoms) has likewise been attributed to a demand for such protective shields for the guiltful or self-conscious soul. Some eye surgeons,[5] more dedicated to the psychoanalytical approach, have indeed regarded the glass of such spectacles as the symbolic equivalent of the hymen, and hold that the use of virtually plain-glass spectacles indicates a need to retrieve a lost virginity.*

Since the eye is thus the vehicle to sex, blindness is the tra-ditional punishment for sexual licence. Oedipus pierced his eyes after discovering his incest, and the intrusive young men of Sodom were blinded for their alleged designs against the visiting angels. Peeping Tom was blinded through looking at the naked (and exhibitionistic) Godiva; Tiresias the soothsayer had been blinded because he had seen Athene bathing naked; and the threat of blindness was (and in some places still is) the age-old deterrent to the masturbating schoolboy. The hysterical belief in the

---

*More than half of the American population over the age of five wear glasses and, of these, women outnumber men in every category. Sometimes these spectacles are justified by the wearer on the basis of the myth that the eye can be damaged by not wearing glasses or by wearing incorrect ones. In fact the eye itself can never be damaged in this way. The only occasion where glasses may help to prevent impairment of sight is in the rare amblyopia (usually from a squint) in small children, where the lowered vision is due to changes in the brain (comparable to hysterical blindness) and not in the eye.

damaging effects of sexual incontinence a century ago is as incomprehensible now as the equivalent fear of witchcraft in the centuries that went before; and it is chastening to find this obsession spelt out in a fourteen-page article in the reputable *Archives of*

Oedipus putting out his eyes.

Ophthalmology of 1882 entitled 'Eye Diseases and Masturbation'.[6] Six years later the Bowman Lecture to the Ophthalmological Society of the United Kingdom[7] explains at length how masturbation can produce amblyopia, retinal haemorrhage, follicular inflammation, catarrh, trachoma, retinal irritation, neuro-retinitis (in young ladies) and total blindness, not to mention agoraphobia

St Lucy, the patron saint of ophthalmology.

and other more bizarre sequels. And even in 1964 we still find a Professor of Ophthalmology[8] citing as one of the nine causes of defective eyesight an 'excess of sexual appetite'! Schizophrenics, burdened with sex-guilt, have on many occasions removed either their testicles or their eyes, as vehicles for their shameful needs. And St Lucy, the patron saint of ophthalmology, tore out both her eyeballs, because she had looked on a man lustfully. (God, in His wisdom, then gave her two replacements.)*

The most curious and widespread development of this relationship between God, the eye, and sex is found in the concept of the Evil Eye – one of the oldest and most prevalent superstitions in history, reaching from ancient Assyria† to present-day Sicily, and from India to Peru, with the swastika constantly reappearing as

St Odilia nursing her new, but over-large, eyeballs.

*The Scottish equivalent, St Triduana, sent her offending eyes on a skewer to her lustful admirer, and the Irish equivalent, St Medana, plucked out her eyes and threw them at the feet of her lover. St Odilia, like St Lucy, was miraculously given two replacements; but unfortunately so large that she had to carry them round like a handbag.

†King Ashurbanapal of Nineveh (668–626 BC) had incantations available with which he could combat the dangerous glances of his Assyrian witches.

the protecting symbol. The Evil Eye was generally a perquisite of women until the last century, when it was even attributed to popes (such as Pius IX and Leo XIII) and to kings (such as Alfonso XIII) and, with perhaps more excuse, to poets like Lord Byron. Irish school-children are still frightened of encountering the single lethal eye of the giant Balor, legendary King of the Formorians. Like the Roman god, Janus, the Hindu god Siva had an evil third

The god Siva.

eye in the centre of his forehead; this was normally kept closed, as it would burn up anything it looked at, whereas the Medusa's turned all to stone. The basilisk (a sort of hooded cobra) and the cockatrice (which had been incubated by a toad from the egg of an elderly cock) were the animal equivalents.★

★Roger Bacon (1214–99) tells how Alexander the Great once attacked a city defended by a basilisk on its walls; advised by Aristotle, he used a large polished surface to reflect the poisonous glance and destroy the serpent. But to most authorities, even the mirror could reflect the damaging rays. Sir Thomas Browne believed that Evil Eyes could even transmit infections when reflected from a mirror; and authorities such as Pliny, St Thomas Aquinas and Roger Bacon knew that the mirror was always dulled by such a glance – a diagnostic test that was freely used to expose witches and criminals.

Throughout its history the evil eye (like witchcraft) has always been related to sex, both in the 'caster' and the recipient. As Antony of Carthagena (1611) said, 'Old women can fascinate more easily because the menstrual blood is retained in their veins,' and the glance of a menstruating woman is believed by South African bushmen to turn men into trees, and among certain American Indians, menstruating women are required to leave the

A cockatrice, after Leonardo.

camp, the only antidote to their glances being to protect oneself behind the forefingers crossed in the pattern of a swastika.* In the recipient, the especial power of the evil eye was to destroy fertility, with periods of particular vulnerability at the sexual climacterics of circumcision, puberty, marriage and childbirth.[9]

Small wonder, then, that throughout history the blind have

*The Caduceus, carried by Mercury, was also a protecting symbol, initially designed to shield him from the evil eye of Juno. By a confusion with the emblem of Aesculapius (a single serpent on a staff), it was adopted as the badge of the medical profession by Sir William Butts, physician to King Henry VIII.

been regarded as damned, paying the penalty for some sexual failing – in themselves, or in their fathers before them, or, among Hindus, of their previous incarnations. As such, they were relegated to the lowest social status, any attempt to better them being held as an impious intervention in God's judgement.

Rarely in history was a humane thought given to the armies of blind beggars that languished in every kingdom. Sometimes they were execrated, as in the edict of King David, who said, 'Whosoever getteth up to the father, and smiteth the Jebusites, and the lame and the blind, that are hated of David's soul, He shall be Chief and Captain' (II Samuel, 5:8). Other despots simply augmented their number, such as the Byzantine Emperor Basil, 'The Bulgar-Slayer', who sent back his 15,000 prisoners, every man blinded, to their king (who died of the shock). And in England blinding was introduced in AD 600 as an alternative to the death penalty.

Thus the blind remained through history as ineducable mendicants, who only came to the fore when their sightless eyes were replaced by an inner vision. The famous soothsayers of history and fable have, in the main, had their prophetic eyes liberated by their blindness. As Milton put it: *Blind Thamyris* (p. 128) *and blind Meonides* [Homer] *And Tiresia and Phineus, prophets old.* To these may be added Blind Bartimeus, who recognized Jesus as Messiah, 'Capys, the sightless seer', who inspired Romulus, and Appius Claudius, who warned the Roman Senate of disaster if they came to terms with Pyrrhus. Democritus, the laughing philosopher of Abdera, even eviscerated his eyes so that he might think more clearly, and this was the practice of some muezzins, who, after learning the Koran by heart, thus ensured that they could not be distracted by beauty. Indeed a similar pseudo-castration was suggested by certain Fathers of the Church, on the grounds that a vision of the next world was preferable to vision in this.[10] Wotan, who drank from Mimir's fountain in order to become the wisest of gods, had to sacrifice one eye in the process. (Wagner, perhaps subconsciously adding the sexual motif, gave Wotan his wife Fricka as a further (questionable) recompense for the loss of his eye.) Horus, who had lost an eye in his fight with Set, had it restored by Thoth, the God of Wisdom: thus his eye became the symbol of sacrifice and acquired magical powers, and was

Wotan in Die Walküre.

A harpist playing before Horus.

established as a hallmark of the medical profession which we acknowledge with the opening symbol ℞ in each prescription we write.

Milton, indeed, believed that his own insight was increased by his loss of vision, and Dr Pierre Villey,[11] himself blind, writes:

There is more equilibrium and judgment with the gifted blind man than with the man who can see. This is not surprising, for sight is the sense for amusement. The less one is disturbed thus, the less one's inner thoughts are interrupted by outward events, the more one is concentrated on oneself, the more time one takes to ripen one's reflections and to weigh the for-and-against of one's deliberations.

James Thurber, after he lost his sight, said:

A blind man benefits by lack of distractions; my one-eighth vision happily obscures sad and ungainly sights, leaving only the vivid and the radiant, some of whom are my friends and neighbours.

Soon after becoming blind, the author, Booth Tarkington, remarked:

I have done more work during the past year than ever before. I have written a novel, short stories, and several essays. Being unable to see is a great aid to concentration. You are not distracted. Half of people's appetite is a result of looking at food. Now I can't see what I'm eating, I feel I could very easily dispense with it.

Psychology and Art of the Blind

Although St Louis had let humanity prevail when he founded the 'Quinze-Vingts' in 1260 (which is still functioning as the 'Asile des Aveugles'), it was not until the advent of the Enlightenment in the late eighteenth century that the possibility of assisting, educating and even curing the blind was seriously considered. Louis Braille suggested his revolutionary script in 1835 (originally as an aid to blind musicians), although it was thirty years in gaining acceptance; and after that the blessings of the mechanical age poured in, until now, with talking-books, typewriters, radio, cassettes, telephones and a hundred other devices, a useful and rewarding life is at last within their reach. Along with all this came a widespread curiosity about the psychology of the blind, for whom new hospitals, charities and societies were emerging. This interest was heightened by the impact of Freudian lore, which established the peculiar importance of our eyes and sight in the evolution of our personalities. Until the turn of the century, there were constant references to the blind man's development of extra senses that could divine colours in cloth, project the sense of touch beyond arm's length, and make it possible to feel radiations that ordinary mortals never know. Indeed the more fanciful of the blind – perhaps in whimsy, perhaps in despair – would sometimes encourage these investigations by talking of the obscure skin contractions experienced as they approached obstacles. But reason gradually prevailed and it became apparent that the blind did little more than concentrate their attention and awareness.*The old concept is, nevertheless, far from dead in the popular mind, and the recent publicity given to Rosa Kuleshova who claimed to recognize colours and read print through her fingertips – even when felt through layers of metal or glass – gave an impetus to that improbable theory of 'dermo-optical perception' which had been floated by Jules Romains some forty years ago.[12] Rosa subsequently found that she could read equally well through her toes, and then through

---

*It is true that light-sensitive pigments are present in the skin of many animals, mainly aquatic forms with non-waterproof skins; but such a dermal light-sense is very rare in terrestrial arthropods, cephalopods and amniotes. These pigment spots have no fundamental difference from true eyes, with which they may co-exist (having similar photo-chemical systems), and they may serve to control locomotion, even in some lower vertebrates.

The formal explanation of Rosa's cutaneous photo-sensitivity was that it was associated with the ability of nerve-endings in her skin to record chemical changes from light in the form of a mosaic, for it was found that this sensitivity could be lowered by careful washing and extraction of the carotenoids from her stratum corneum. American investigators have postulated other pigments, possibly enhanced by melanin, differential penetration of differing wave-lengths, and so on.[14] None of these carries great conviction, especially since Greisbach and Kunz measured the sensory acuity of a respectable number of blind children in France and Germany and concluded that the loss of a major sense impairs rather than increases the acuity of the others. A more recent survey by Ewart, who tested the tactile recognition of form in thirty blind and thirty sighted children, showed no significant difference except when the children had a high I.Q., in which case they were materially more successful than their sighted colleagues.[15]

her elbow. These claims were later exposed, but others had meanwhile taken her cue; in the USSR she was followed by Ninel Kulagina and Lena Bliznova, and even in sceptical New York, twenty girls from Barnard College joined the ranks of the dermo-optical perceivers.[13] Others have followed, but somehow the world remains unconvinced, and no evidence has been found of thermal and textural clues on which this egregious capacity could be based.

The notion that our other senses are enhanced by our blindness is still well-established in relation to hearing, and even to smell, for we know that blind camel-drivers are highly esteemed, since the smell of the earth gives guidance in the desert where sight is often of little avail.

In general, the established blind betray a patient scepticism when determined psychologists attempt to dissect their attitudes, categorize their failings and generalize about their special psychopathology. They say (with justice) that they are but ordinary men with the ordinary proportions of personality patterns, to whom blindness is just an inconvenient accident. Margery Fry's comment,[16] that 'to the administrator an individual may be just "that old woman: I think her name is Jones", but to herself she is Katie Jones who won a prize for scripture and had the smallest waist in her class – with a thousand other distinctive features – who just happens to be old', applies with equal force to the blind and partially-sighted population.*

Nevertheless, these diverse personalities tend to be given a cloak of uniformity, fashioned partly by our concept of how a blind person should behave and partly by the blind person's own acceptance of an attitude that seems appropriate to the minority group to which he belongs. Thus, just as we generalize about the volatile Frenchman, the stolid Teuton and the operatic Italian, so we have our ready image of the heroic† or pathetic blind; and

---

*One recalls the garden of specially scented flowers created in 1968 in Regents Park, London, for the delectation of the blind (their Institute lies hard-by). The intent was not well received, blind commentators emphasizing that their main wish was to be integrated into society as inconspicuously as possible, and that they had little interest in these gardens which would merely serve to accentuate their segregation.

†Sometimes his heroism is carried almost to excess, as in the case of John, the blind king of Bohemia, who bravely led his troops on the field of Crécy; or Blind Bayard, the legendary steed given to Rinaldo by Charlemagne, which is still apparently to be heard neighing and snorting in the Ardennes on Midsummer Night.

into this mould we tend to press the blind personalities we meet, so that the blind man is inevitably drawn to act up to his established image.

To the more sensitive psyche this rather spurious rôle may seem distasteful and, if the blind person has not the discipline and forbearance to maintain his integrity, he may well relapse into a vegetable existence within his sheltered employment, or even withdraw, a little soured or defiant, into a world of his own. Happily these negative or antisocial responses are rare, because the blind man is forced to open himself to his fellows; he is dependent on their conversation and help for nearly everything he does. Privacy is difficult to sustain when one's most intimate actions may well need supervision if not actual assistance, or indeed may be observed without one's knowledge. The blind man tends to become increasingly responsive, since his whole orientation depends on constant communication with his fellows; should he start as an intelligent introvert, this secondary extroversion that he accomplishes may yield a personality-amalgam approaching the ideal.

This situation contrasts strikingly with the predicament of the deaf, whose difficulty in communication forces them to retreat into a world of their own. Resentment at the evident embarrassment their company causes is combined with suspicion that they are being deceived or maligned in the conversations they cannot comprehend; and a secondary introversion furthers their retreat. Small wonder that the blind are popular. They excite sympathy and admiration, and they figure again and again in literature as repositories for our sentimental needs, while one would search long to find a hero or heroine in fiction who was deaf or dumb.

When the sight is suddenly lost, there will inevitably follow a period in which shock, despair, defiance, over-compensation and acceptance succeed one another. Thereafter it is just a matter of making the extra efforts of awareness and adaptation, and learning to live within one's new confines. It is the limitation of physical freedom that is perhaps the most exacting, for few blind people ever venture beyond the safety of their home or place of work. Yet they rarely yearn for the recovery of their sight. Once these adjustments have been made, they find it hard to face the further battle of re-adapting to a seeing world. J. F. Wilson[17] described how he was once subjected to some tests based on Romains' theory that pigment spots within the skin can be developed as a substitute for normal vision. He says that he desisted, 'not because these tests appeared tiresome and unproductive, but because concentration on the prospect of regaining my sight caused me a good deal of mental disturbance'. He also quoted one of his blind colleagues who, at the age of sixteen, refused to cooperate in treatment which might have brought him some sight, simply because he could not face the consequences of its success.

Whereas those who once had good sight will retain through their years of blindness a concept of space, distance, colours and perspective, even if these become rendered down and formalized as time passes, the blind-from-birth can conceive objects only in terms of three dimensions, embellished by qualities of texture and significance. Such a conception is usually stable and precise, admitting little ambiguity or illusion.★

As Wilson puts it, 'The primary object of a tactual conception must necessarily be small enough to be felt. Blind people differ in their ability to correlate single tactual concepts imaginatively into something like a tactual "scene". Undoubtedly, some are able to build up a tri-dimensional picture of a very large object from its single, feelable components'; and he quotes the following lines from a poem entitled *Touch Landscape* by the late W. H. Coates,[18] who was blind from birth, as a remarkable example of that ability exceptionally developed:

Then stepped my fancy out over the scene.
Through stiff bracken she waded,
The turf caressed her feet.
The ground flowed away in broad slopes towards the valley.

She heard the shadow-sound of trees;
Her hands brushed the fields – a thousand acres –
To touch the distant wood
Flung like a scarf of lace
Upon the knees of the hills.

★Diderot gives the following comment from his blind companion: 'If it were not for curiosity, I would just as soon have long arms; it seems to me my hands would tell me more of what goes on in the moon than your eyes or your telescopes; and, besides, eyes cease to see sooner than hands to touch.'

She buried her face in grasses rich and cool
When to the plain she leapt
Beside a level river —
A polished strip of metal cutting the pastures.

And thence to farther hills
Swelling beneath my disembodied hands
In three-dimensional curves:
Most lovely hills, phantom and far away
And overlaid with velvet.

And farther yet, beyond the misty hills,
I reached the wrinkled sea;
I touched the waves with crests of thistledown.

Objects too large to be encompassed by the hands and arms are more often conceived by a process of imagination which reduces them to touchable size, or by the blind subject projecting himself, as it were, into the situation conceived. These two methods are exemplified by the following answers from two men blind from birth, when asked by Wilson how they would picture a battleship shooting at an attacking aeroplane. The 'reducer' replied: 'At first my mind will register only a confusion of noises such as the BBC Effects Department would produce for such an occasion. But, when I get past that, I find that what I am actually doing is something like producing a puppet show. The battleship, a spiky toy affair, such as I played with in my bath as a child, and the aeroplane diving to the attack in proportion. I am following its descent with my cupped hands as I might the flight of a wasp.' The 'projector' replied: 'I don't conceive the whole thing, such as a battleship, ever. It's more the case of me on the bridge, me in a turret, me walking along a corridor below the water-line. Picturing a train, I may occasionally think of it as a trembling arrow of sound that hurls itself through the station, setting everything a-quiver and gone in a flash. More often it would be me in a compartment with no sense of the whole train beyond the rhythm and movement of the carriage.'

Of these two responses, the first permits but a weak grasp of objective reality, whereas the second can hardly be called objective at all. Both are sadly lacking in the grandeur and richness of visual imagery.

Wilson also quotes another of Coates' (unpublished) poems as the most successful attempt he knows to translate visual terms into tactile imagery. Here Coates has taken a stanza from Shelley's *Prometheus Unbound* (in which the nymph Asia is watching the dawn break over the mountains), which is loaded with visual images; nevertheless the tactile vocabulary never fails, and the result is far above the simple exercise of a translator's skill:

Shelley (*Prometheus Unbound*, Act II, line 19):

> *The point of one white star is quivering still*
> *Deep in the orange light of widening morn*
> *Beyond the purple mountains: through a chasm*
> *Of wind-divided mist the darker lake*
> *Reflects it; now it wanes: it gleams again*
> *As the waves fade, and as the burning threads*
> *Of woven cloud unravel in pale air:*
> *'Tis lost! And through yon peaks of cloudlike snow*
> *The roseate sunlight quivers: . . .*

Coates' 'translation':

> *One cold metallic grain is quivering still*
> *Deep in the flood of warm ethereal fluid*
> *Beyond the velvet mountains: through a chasm*
> *In banks of fleece the heavier lake is splashed*
> *With flakes of fiery foam; it wanes: it grows*
> *As the waves thicken, and as the burning threads*
> *Of woven wool unravel in tepid air;*
> *'Tis lost! And through the unsubstantial snow*
> *Of yonder peaks quivers the living form*
> *And vigour of the sun: . . .*

This verbal imagery of the blind has all the fascination of an Alice-in-Wonderland world, where everything is strange yet recognizable and true, and sometimes no less beautiful. But it would be wrong to infer that much blind writing is of this high order; the blind have little chance to comprehend the beauties and subtleties of sighted literature, whose references and images must so often be without meaning, and they have had no tradition of tactile-writing on which to build their style or from which to furnish their stock of symbols. For the blind, our vocabulary has been stripped of many of its richest descriptive words and phrases, and none have been added in their place. In learning to keep afloat in a bustling, sighted world, so much else must be mastered, so much extra time and effort is absorbed by the simplest tasks, that the energy to create new symbols and metaphors, and to learn how best to deploy them, is more than can be expected of all but the fortunate and gifted few.

It would be a pity to leave the literature of the blind without reference to the most famous of all blind poets – Homer. But the theory of his blindness is based very insecurely on a single 'Homeric hymn', in which the writer speaks personally of himself as 'a blind man, and he lives in rocky Chios'. It is supported (equally insecurely) by Homer's sparse and apparently con- tradictory use of visual images and colour names (e.g. black [μέλαν] is applied to blood, new-ploughed earth, water, ships, wine, and so on); but this seeming confusion is common in Greek literature. However, some further support for the existence of a 'blind Homer' has recently been claimed by psychological analysis of Homer's dream sequences, which are declared to carry the same elements and follow the same patterns as do the dreams of the blind, indicating that Homer lost his sight at an early age[19] (his visual similes do contradict this view). In fact, blind poets rarely compose long or complex poems. Milton was the excep- tion, partly because his long-suffering daughter was unique. The Argentinian poet Borges,[20] describing how his blindness had forced him to abandon story writing and return to short poems (usually in classical form – 'because rhyme has a mnemonic value'), explained that 'a sonnet is a "Thing", as it were. I can go on walking all over the town, while I carry a sonnet in my head, polishing and altering as I go. You can't do that with a long piece of prose.'

In musical composition, the same sort of problems and physical impediments face the blind as in creative writing, unless, of course, the blindness comes on only in middle life, as in the case of Delius or, in old age, with both Bach and Handel who, like their literary counterpart Milton, had reached their creative maturity in a sighted world. Both Bach[21] and Handel[22] had their cataracts removed by the arch-charlatan Chevalier Taylor, surgeon-oculist to the Princess of Wales, who failed to restore sight in either of them.* When Handel was grieving that blindness robbed him of any power to compose, it was suggested that he might be assisted by John Stanley, the distinguished composer and organist who had been blinded in infancy.[23] The blind do often make excellent musicians, but the difficulty of reading by touch and memorizing a score usually limits their prowess to a solo *tour de force*, or to accompanying their own songs – like the blind Demodocus, who beguiled Odysseus as he lingered at the court of Alcinous.

For the blind who are creative, painting would seem to be excluded, at any rate for those whose loss of sight is complete, unless they feel a compulsive desire to deploy a lingering memory of colour values – perhaps reinforced by symbolism or synaesthesia. Last year the New York Academy of Sciences exhibited twenty-three abstract 'Dreamscapes' by Crist Delmonico, a thirty-year-old who had been blind since unsuccessful cataract surgery at fourteen; his spinning, geometrical shapes served as background to a complexity of colours which he used with an expressionistic fervour ('like dancing'). However, to the large majority of the blind, sculpture can at least provide an ample outlet.

In the last chapter we noted how a gradual restriction of the field of vision could sometimes liberate the young artist from the constraints imposed by a convention that required a near-photographic likeness of the subject he was trying to depict, and allowed him increasingly to emphasize the features that were to him most relevant. The blind artist, having no such constraint, can express his feelings for the subject as soon as he has learnt to control his medium.

The next illustration shows very well the three stages in evolution of the sculpture of a boy who had been blind from birth, and compare interestingly with the drawings of the partially sighted boy (p. 149). He starts with the sculptural equivalent of that first crudely realistic stage (although the head in this case is

---

*In fact both were probably blind from another cause. As well as being clinically irresponsible, Taylor's accounts (such as his assertion that he also de-cataracted Edward Gibbon) cannot be trusted and Handel's cataract had previously been cleared by William Bramfield at St George's Hospital. All of these operations were done by the time-honoured 'couching' technique (dislocating the cataractous lens away from the pupil with a needle), which had been practised since about 3000 BC; this gave way only slowly to the 'extraction' which Daviel had devised in 1748, and couching is still a common practice in many rural areas of the third world.

Sculpture by a congenitally blind boy: stages in development (Lowenfeld[24]).

fashioned facing away from its creator). This is followed by the same second stage of structural discovery, with great over-emphasis of the seemingly significant features, vaguely geometrical, and equivalent to neolithic art in many of its more mature representations. And there is the same final stage, when the blind sculptor freely expresses his experiences by introducing new elements of form, or by varying his own structural symbols.

The concept of an autonomous 'haptic' sense, that allows the apprehension of form and space independently of optics and acoustics, is not difficult to accept, and this may simply lie buried beneath the visual assessment in all but those who are born blind. But (as V. Lowenfeld has maintained)[24] for a minority, the haptic sense remains the primary orientation. Such people interpret their world by touch, by their bodily feelings and by their muscular sensations, and their art is thus essentially 'expressionistic', in contrast to the visually motivated majority who tend to paint in a more realistic style.

The awareness that this separate haptic evaluation may have its own aesthetic came to the fore after the First World War, when a group of French sculptors recommended blindfolding in order to emphasize the three-dimensional quality of their renderings by excluding all visual perception. Thereafter the totally blind were encouraged to express themselves in sculpture, and the images that have been produced during the ensuing decades are full of interest and appeal. But there is still the essential question of whether the achievements of blind sculptors are determined by

Exhibition of Arts for blind people.

autonomous haptic principles, or correspond to our own aesthetic norms; and this problem (in spite of the extensive investigations of G. Révész)[25] remains unanswered.

Just as the fundamental basis of aesthetics still remains an enigma, the whole underlying pattern of how we integrate our percepts is still far from solved. This latter issue has long excited interest among philosophers, and since philosophy in the grand sense no longer exists, psychoanalysts, replacing the lapidary language of Locke by a formidable jargon of their own, have sustained the inquiry with redoubled zest.

Locke[26] had first raised this issue in 1690 when, based on the observations of his blind Dublin companion, Molyneux, he decided that the idea of space must be a simple idea that could be indiscriminately 'let into the mind' either by sight or touch – or by both simultaneously. Such a unitary concept was questioned by Berkeley[27] (in his *New Theory of Vision*) in 1709, who argued that sight was truly concerned only with 'light and colours' and

(a)   (b)

Sculptures by a blind girl: (a) Deserted *(b)* Mourning.

our notions of space were acquired solely from the moving, extended bodies 'in circumambient space'; and although Locke's view generally prevailed, it now seems that Berkeley reached nearer to the truth. It could be added that in Eastern Europe the

Sculpture by a blind girl: Women Talking.

motor theory (that 'Touch teaches Vision') prevails, since it is found more compatible with Marxist–Leninist philosophy. Nevertheless, our vision dominates our touch, even re-shaping it; and, when the two are in conflict, vision wins.[28]

The Recovery of Sight

The recovery of sight, and the complex process by which a man, born blind and well adapted in a world of touch and sound, learns to re-evaluate his world in terms of sight, is one that has always fascinated those who have witnessed its slow evolution. It has, incidentally, provided a frequent *coup-de-théâtre* for novels, films and stage, particularly since the advent of corneal grafting. Such fictional accounts were not bothered with the need for accuracy, as the dramatic moment required an almost immediate recognition of all one's surroundings, and in particular of all the more romantic members of the cast.

The first scientific assessment of how one 'learns to see' was made by the pioneer eye-surgeon, William Cheselden,[29] in the *Philosophical Transactions* of 1728; to his account, exemplary in its clarity and concision, the rather archaic phraseology of his time lends an added charm, which makes it difficult to resist quoting him at some length:

An account of observations made by a young gentleman who was born blind, or lost his sight so early that he had no remembrance of ever having seen, and was couch'd between thirteen and fourteen years of age.

... who, though he knew these colours asunder in a good light, yet when he saw them after he was couch'd, the faint ideas he had of them before, were not sufficient for him to know them by afterwards, and therefore he did not think them the same which he had before known by those names. Now scarlet he thought the most beautiful of all colours, and of others the most gay were the most pleasing; whereas the first time he saw black it gave him great uneasiness, yet after a little time he was reconciled to it; but some months after, seeing by accident a Negro woman, he was struck with great horror at the sight.

When he first saw, he was so far from making any judgment about distances, that he thought all objects whatever touch'd his eyes (as he express'd it) as what he felt did his skin, and thought no objects so agreeable as those which were smooth and regular, though he could form no judgment of their shape, or guess what it was in any object that was pleasing to him: He knew not the shape of any thing, nor any one thing from another, however different in shape or magnitude; but upon being told what things were, whose form he before knew from feeling, he would carefully observe, that he might know them again; but having too many objects to learn at once, he forgot many of them; and (as he said) at first he learned to know, and again forgot a thousand things in a day. One particular only, though it may appear trifling, I will relate: Having often forgot which was the cat, and which the dog, he was asham'd to ask; but catching the cat, which he knew by feeling, he was observed to look at her steadfastly, and then, setting her down, said, So, puss, I shall know you another time ... We thought he soon knew what pictures represented, which were shew'd to him, but we found afterwards we were mistaken; for about two months after he was couch'd, he discovered at once they represented solid bodies, when to that time he considered them only as party-colour'd planes, or surfaces diversified with a variety of paint; ...

Being shewn his father's picture in a locket in his mother's watch, and told what it was, he acknowledged a likeness, but was vastly surprised; asking, how could it be, that a large face could be express'd in so little room; saying, it should have seemed as impossible to him, as to put a bushel of any thing into a pint. . . .

A year after first seeing, being carried upon Epsom Downs, and observing a large prospect, he was exceedingly delighted with it, and called it a new kind of seeing. And now being lately couch'd of his other eye, he says, that objects at first appeared large to this eye, but not so large as they did at first to the other; and looking upon the same object with both eyes, he thought it looked about twice as large as with the first couch'd eye only, but not double, that we can any ways discover.

After Cheselden, two further accounts were published, also in the *Philosophical Transactions* – by James Ware in 1810[30] and James Wardrop in 1826.[31]

The first was an account of a boy ('Master W, the son of a respectable clergyman at Castlecary ...') whom Ware saw when only six months of age, with rather large eyes that looked off-centre, and cataracts were then discerned within the pupils. Surgery was deferred till he was eight, and the boy's experiences differed little from those recorded by Cheselden, except that objects were not thought to be 'touching the eye' but projected to an arm's range away, and colours presented no problem (he had doubtless seen more than was admitted previously).

Then James Wardrop presented his 'first report of recovery at an advanced age' (actually forty-six). The lady had had successive operations on both eyes in infancy (her Parisian doctors were too impatient), presumably for congenital cataracts; one eye was promptly destroyed by infection and its fellow left with a doubtful projection of light. Twelve days after Wardrop's third division of her 'occluded pupil', she was first allowed out of her darkened room, 'into the Piazza of Covent Garden, when she expressed surprise and delight at the blue colour of the sky'. All colours were a confusing novelty, with a strong preference for yellow, and then pink; distances beyond an arm's length, and judgements of all shapes and size, were also difficult to comprehend, albeit clear (the small artificial pupil evidently gave her pin-hole vision which compensated for the absence of any lens).

Since these reports there have been over fifty accounts of the recovery of sight, illustrating the translation of an orientation from an essentially haptic and auditory world into one subservient to the retinal image; and the story is always much the same.

The sixteen best-documented of these case-reports were recently analysed by C. M. Fisher.[32] Their ages ranged from seven to forty-six, and most of them had had time to enjoy a sufficiently rich and complex perceptual experience relating to the size, shape and significance of objects, as determined by other sensory means. Without exception, they had the greatest difficulty in relating the three dimensions they knew from touch to the new two-dimensional image they saw; as in the case of Cheselden's boy, it was months before they were able to accept that the three-dimensional actuality could be amply registered by a two-dimensional picture. Colours were always a problem, for the emotional tones that had previously been developed to give them 'labels' were difficult to adjust to the reality (cf. Locke's blind friend, to whom scarlet signified something 'like the sound of a trumpet'), although the colours could often be registered before the actual forms of the objects they decked, but without having any spatial localization, after the manner of smells.

At first all things were imagined to be touching the eyes, and it was an effort to push them, as it were, back into perspective. In consequence, everything seemed very large, but it was difficult to conceive of objects (such as mountains) being even larger than they actually looked. Vertical and horizontal dimensions were hard to relate. The fields of vision seemed constricted, as the crude image and colours from the peripheral retina were at first too confusing to assess. All the cases had a poor visual memory and a poor capacity for localizing sound.

It was also difficult to relate movements of hand or eye to the newly seen world: the eyes tended to wander from the object they were trying to inspect, and moved clumsily in the directions to which they were commanded; the pointing finger went awry, and the hands and arms could not indicate the dimensions of familiar objects.

In short, seeing a thing is not an innate and automatic capacity. Every element of what is called 'perception' – line, curve, angle, direction, outline, shape, shadow, form – had to be recognized and acquire meaning. Fisher's conclusion, that perception is not a process separable from recognition, was echoed in the very extensive survey (of sixty-five cases) by von Senden,[33] who had set out to determine whether the blind from birth have a sense of space, with which a new-found sight can readily be integrated.

It would indeed be interesting to expose such a newly seeing patient to a truly abstract painting (eschewing representation altogether and dealing entirely with colours – a view which ought to have the qualities of his own natural world), and to encourage him to paint before the interpretation of his colours and shapes begins to sully the 'purity' of his vision.

Before cataract implants became established, it was a commonplace among eye-doctors that elderly patients, whose sight had been restored by surgery, were often among the least grateful. Many had relaxed into a protected and undemanding vegetable life, which was rudely upset by being expected to fend for themselves. They had to learn to see through their new 'pebble' glasses, which distorted the view, and made straight lines bent, and this curved outside world then squirmed about with every movement of the eyes like writhing snakes that never stayed still; while in ordinary conversations, faces popped in and out of the encircling blind area with the annoying insolence of a jack-in-the-box. Many a successful operation was thwarted by a frail psyche that preferred to grope its way through life, rather than cope with this formidable new visual world.

No wonder such older patients are often found to remain 'behaviourally blind', in spite of recovering relatively good sight, and continue to assess the world by touch and hearing; prolonged training in visual rehabilitation is sometimes called for, but is effective only if started soon afterwards, when the level of motivation is high.

The personal problems of 'learning to see' can often be overwhelming, as the patient may need to shut his eyes again and again, in order to retreat into the security of the sightless world he knows, before resuming the struggle to reassemble his new world, making little or no use of his customary methods of apprehending tactile impressions. His personal life takes on entirely new forms; it is brought home to him how much other people can observe him without laying a hand on him; and he realizes that he must take an interest in his clothes, attend to his hair and watch how other people regard him. He gives up many habits that he could not formerly relinquish, because he is suddenly ashamed of them. He also acquires for the first time an interest in objects and a desire to possess them, that may lead to dissimulation, envy, theft and fraud, and at other times evoke an aesthetic interest that has never been experienced before.

At the end of all this comes the inevitable question – is it really worth it? – when we suggest a sight-restoring operation to a man who, blind from birth, has established for himself a satisfactory orientation and way of life. One recalls the sorry case of Sidney Bradford,[34] whose corneal opacities (the sequel to infantile vaccination) were grafted away at the age of fifty-two. He found that the transfer from touch to vision proved quite easy, and the minimum of training allowed him to read letters which he had come to know only by touch. Nevertheless, he soon became dispirited; he found the world drab, and was upset by flaking paint and other blemishes; he liked bright colours, but became depressed when the light faded. And this cheerful, well-adjusted man, with a useful industrial job, who was happily reading Braille in his spare time before the operation, became deeply disturbed thereafter, and, losing his self-respect, soon died in unhappiness. The moral of this story should not be lightly overlooked.

Envoy

Perhaps I have wandered, in this last chapter, rather far off the road on which we first set forth. For the response to total blindness is many-sided, and involves us in wider issues, to which I could do scant justice. Nevertheless the artistry of the blind, which cannot really be appreciated outside the framework of the blind environment, is at least a crystallization of the world they experience; and of this world the limited visual impediments discussed in the earlier chapters can be held to provide several reflections.

From the diverse interpretations that I have assembled in this book, the reader must accept or reject what he fancies, because by their very nature they can never be wholly established or wholly rejected. In the main they stem from the wave of iconoclasm at the turn of the century; and, once a mechanistic basis for all spiritual and aesthetic experiences had been suggested, all sorts of theories became stuck like burrs on to the accommodating body of this hypothesis, which are naturally suspect in the critical climate of today. But they are none the worse for an airing; for in some of them there are truths that could be worth pursuing.

APPENDIX

1

Thus R. D. Palmer[1] determined that those with impaired vision were calmer and less excitable, seeking low levels of activation and 'stimulus input'. Stevens and Wolff[2] found that myopic freshmen made significantly better college entrance grades, were more introverted in the thinking and social areas, were more likely to be emotionally inhibited, disinclined to motor-activity and to social leadership and formed more highly differentiated memory schemata. While Young's[3] more recent analysis of college students showed that whereas the myopes are significantly more orientated towards *abasement* (feeling and accepting guilt), the non-myopes are significantly more given to *exhibition* (wanting to be the centre of attention, talking of their achievements) and to feeling the need for *change* (impatient with the daily routine). Less significantly, the myopes rated more highly in *achievement* (the need to do one's best), *intraception* (analysing one's own and others' feelings), *succorance* (needing help from others when in trouble) and *heterosexuality*; while the non-myopes showed a greater need for *order* and for *dominance* (the need to be leader of the group).

A third analysis of male students by Becker[4] showed that those with refractive errors had higher scores on *application* and *endurance*, but less than the normal-sighted on *achievement*. He also reported the curious finding of a higher proportion of these ametropes among the first-born.

2

H. Osborne[5] summarizes the colour concepts of the ancient Greeks thus. They were not given to careful discrimination of colour hue, and there is little evidence of attention to hues except possibly within the violet-purple band. The Greek colour-vocabulary was jejune, and the available terms were bunched into a small number of groups. Within each group the terms did not differentiate in virtue of hue, but were used indifferently as synonyms or differentiated in respect of brightness and intensity. In their literature the Greeks used words signifying black, white, grey, green, blue-purple, yellow-orange and red, each with a number of alternative names that probably relate to different degrees of brightness; indeed in the dramas there are only the most elementary references to colour, and then usually referring to brightness rather than hue. From their specific writings on colour, black, white, red and light green were regarded as the primaries by Democritus, while Aristotle thought that the rainbow had only three essential colours – red, green and blue.

In their paintings the ancient Greeks traditionally used only three colours (black, white and red), to which yellow was later added (according to Roman writers, by Polygnotus between 475 and 440 BC), but many other pigments and dyes were in fact available and used. They were far more concerned with saturation and brightness than with hue, and it is probable that fairly violent colours were used lavishly, and without much reference to naturalism, on most of the statuary, but no original paintings of the great period (fifth and fourth century BC) have survived, and it was not until the Augustan period that moderation in the use of colours was achieved.

The common practice of relating specific colour names to specific subjects rather than hues (green-eyed Athene, rosy-fingered dawn, etc.) has continued down to the present in many languages (like Swahili) that are off the mainstream of civilization.

3

'Voyelles' – Rimbaud – (from *Premiers Vers*):

A noir, E blanc, I rouge, U vert, O bleu: voyelles,
Je dirai quelque jour vos naissances latentes:
A, noir corset velu des mouches éclatantes
Qui bombinent autour des puanteurs cruelles,

Golfes d'ombre; E, candeurs des vapeurs et des tentes,
Lances des glaciers fiers, rois blancs, frissons d'ombelles;
I, pourpres, sang craché, rire des lèvres belles
Dans la colère ou les ivresses pénitentes;

U, cycles, vibrements divins des mers virides,
Paix des pâtis semés d'animaux, paix des rides
Que l'alchimie imprime aux grands fronts studieux;

O, suprême Clairon plein de strideurs étranges,
Silences traversés des Mondes et des Anges:
— O l'Oméga, rayon violet de Ses Yeux!

The patient described how with her long vowels, a = 'pink', e = 'rust',
i = 'white', o = 'blue', u = 'dark green'.
Of her musical notes, A = 'peach', C = 'orange/grey', D = 'blue/green',
F = 'yellow', G = 'red'.

In heraldry,

Purple = 'the colour of amethysts, pageantry, royalty and death',
Red = 'the colour of rubies, wine, revelry, furnaces, courage and magic',
Blue = 'the colour of sapphires, deep water, skies, loyalty and melancholy',
Green = 'the colour of emeralds, hope, youth, joy, spring and victory'.

4

Several other instances of colour-defective artists have been described and
analysed. The following account is included, since it is presented from the
slightly different standpoint of a young art-teacher.

One of the students, an extremely quiet and sensitive boy, was about 17 when
he joined my composition class. The first painting he produced, a street scene,
showed a fair sense of arrangement, good drawing, and very unusual colour for a
beginner. He used colours which were bright but not crude, with some red and
yellow, a little green, and a great deal of soft blue and mauve. The general effect
was exciting and pleasing; a change from the usual red, yellow, blue and viridian
in their raw state used by most beginners.

During the following lesson a week later, he asked if he could speak to me
privately, and he then told me that he was completely colour-blind. He said that
he knew which colours to use by the names on the tubes of paint, and that his
difficulty lay in the painting of shadows. Evidently he knew, or had been told,
that there was colour in shadows, but in trying to paint a cool shadow on a warm-
coloured object he could not judge the quantity of the cool pigment he was adding,
and often changed the original colour completely. When I saw his painting again
this was obvious: a red object, for example, might be shaded in blue or purple;
the colour change being so violent that the object was split completely. Although
the colour values were wrong the tone values were so good that they gave the

picture a unity which it would otherwise have completely lacked. All the objects in the composition, as far as I can remember, were painted in their correct colours, blue sky, red roofs, &c.

A colleague tells me that when painting from still life the student later developed a method of working which made up for his colour-blindness. Although the objects he was painting were in front of him (in my class, students worked from memory) he never actually made a mistake in identifying the colour of an object, nor did he ever ask the master to tell him. He may, however, have asked other students. His colour in this class was extremely subdued, quiet and 'safe'; there was nothing wrong with it but its extreme dullness. The form and tone were very good. He had obviously worked out a formula for colour which compensated for whatever defect he had, but which was extremely narrow and incapable of being developed [Cf. Colour Plate VII].

He eventually took up sculpture but I don't believe his work was outstanding.

5

The following (probably irresponsible) account was given by a journalist, in the *New York American* (25 October 1931), entitled 'Louis Wain's fiendish cats', after Wain had been in mental hospital seven years:

Wain, though right-handed in all other things, could draw cats only with his left hand and, until 1925, had produced thousands of delightful drawings of soft pretty agreeable purring pussies – all with his left hand. Then, one day an astonishing thing happened. The artist's right hand, instead of hanging idle, suddenly took the crayon from his left and began drawing cats with a skill quite its equal.

One might not think that would make much difference, but it was enough to drive away the artist's patrons and drive him into a madhouse. The trouble was that all these right-handed cats were different from the lovable left-handed kitties that all cat-lovers had admired. The new ones were fiendish creatures with a hateful light in their eyes, the kind of hell-cats that are supposed to ride on witches' shoulders to the 'Devil's Sabbath'. These were 'crazy cats', and after a struggle to make that right hand behave and give the crayon back to the left, the artist went crazy too.

6

On this replacement basis, the Persian Shah, Aga Mohammed, who had been castrated, took his revenge on society by ordering 30,000 human eyes to be brought to him, which he then counted himself.[6] This ocular projection of sexuality is largely a masculine outlet, since it is the male who traditionally makes the selection of his sexual partner, and is guided in this by the woman's appearance, whereas the woman, traditionally a passive recipient of such attentions, has less occasion to bother about the appearance of the male. And it is the male who principally elaborates his visual fantasies as a sex incentive or substitute (hence the scotophilia, for the actual woman rarely lives up to the appearance of the fantasy one), whereas the female is primarily exhibitionistic and non-cerebral in her sex.

The English, with their nonconformist consciences, and in contrast to the Latins, are said to be largely scotophiliac, preferring their intercourse in the darkness. One recalls the curious finding that when the women attending a provincial hospital were questioned why they had brought their child for circumcision – was it because their husbands were circumcised – a quarter of them did not know the answer, as they had never seen their husbands naked.

7

Further to the comments in Appendix 2 (pp. 180–2), Goethe observed that the Pythagorean brotherhood never mentioned the colour blue; and an absence of both blue and green was noted by Hans Magnus in 1877 on scanning the Bible, the Homeric poems, the hymns of Rig-Veda and the Zend-Avesta. The Latin word *flavus* (pale or golden yellow) evidently became transformed into *blavus* (blue).

REFERENCES

Chapter 1

1 FOSTER, John (1953), 'Curiosa Ophthalmica', *Trans. Ophthal. Soc. Australia*, 12, p. 28.

2 POST, R. H. (1962), 'Population differences in vision acuity', *Eugenics Quarterly*, 9, No. 4, p. 189.

3 RICE, T. (1930), 'Physical defects in Character, II, Near-sightedness', *Hygeia*, 8, p. 644.

4 RICE, T. (1930), 'Physical defects in Character, I, Far-sightedness', *Hygeia*, 8, p. 536.

5 YOUNG, F. A. (1967), 'Myopia and Personality', *Amer. J. Optom.*, 44, p. 192.

6 DOUGLAS, J. W. B., ROSS, J. M. and SIMPSON, H. R. (1968), *All Our Future*, Peter Davies Ltd, London.
DOUGLAS, J. W. B., ROSS, J. M. and SIMPSON, H. R. (1967), 'The ability and attainment of short-sighted pupils', *J. Roy. Stat. Soc.*, Vol. 130, Series A, p. 479.
PECKHAM, C. S., GARDINER, P. A. and GOLDSTEIN, H. (1977), 'Acquired myopia in 11-year-old Children', *Brit. Med. J.*, 1, pp. 542–4.

7 MUELLER, K. (1964), 'The Eyeglasses of Famous Men', *Klin. Mbl. Augenheilk.*, 145, p. 124.

8 AMALRIC, P. (1986), 'Napoléon, était-il myope', *Points de vue*, No. 17 (June), p. 12.

9 HOWARD, P. (1970), *The Royal Palace*, Hamish Hamilton, London, p. 132.

10 RUNCIMAN, S. (1971), personal communication.

11 NAITO, Y. (1966), 'A theory for development of Myopia – Emotion and myopia', *Folia. Ophthal. Jap.*, 17, p. 1131.

12 ALAERTS, Louis (1958), *La Myopie héréditaire des Médicis*, Laboratoires Cusi, Brussels.

13 DESNEUX, Jules (1951), *Rigueur de Jan van Eyck*, Editions des Artistes, Brussels.

14 ROHR, M. von (1923), 'Contributions to the history of the spectacle trade', *Trans. Ophthal. Soc. UK*, 25, p. 44.

15 ALAERTS, op. cit.

16 TENNYSON, Hallam (1897), *Alfred Lord Tennyson, a Memoir*, Macmillan, London.

17 BEATTIE, P. H. (1953), 'The ocular Troubles of Dr Johnson and Mr Pepys', *Proc. Roy. Soc. Med.*, 46, p. 591.

18 SORSBY, A. (1930), 'On the Nature of Milton's Blindness', *Brit. J. Ophthal.*, 14, p. 339.

19 HARDY, W. E. (1934), *Random Reflections on Ophthalmo-Optical History, Techniques, Philosophy, Literature and Personalities*, Hatton Press, London.

20 ORGLER, Hertha (1947), *Alfred Adler and his work*, 2nd ed., Daniel & Co., Rochford, pp. 60, 77–8.

21 MOORMAN, Mary (1965), *William Wordsworth, A Biography – the later years*, Clarendon Press, Oxford, 2, 255.

22 GORMAN, H. (1948), *James Joyce*, Rinehart & Co., NY.
FABRICANT, Noah D. (1957), 'The Ocular History of James Joyce', *E. E. N. T. Monthly*, 36, 731.

23 DOGGART, James H. (1963), 'Gibbon's Eyesight', *Trans. Cambridge Biblio. Soc.*, 3, No. 5, 406.

24 BEATTIE, op. cit.

25 MUELLER, K. (1961), 'Beethoven's Brille', *Klin. Mbl. Augenheilk.*, 138, 412.

26 SCARLETT, E. P. (1964), 'A Doctor comments on Bach', *Arch. Intern. Med. (Chicago)*, 113, 449.

27 SAJNER, J. (1965), 'Gregor Johann Mendel's vision and eyeglasses', *Klin. Mbl. Augenheilk.*, 147, 600.

28 MILLS, L. (1936), 'Peripheral Vision in Art', *Arch. Ophthal. (Chicago)*, 16, 208.

29 SCHAPIRO, M. (1962), *Paul Cézanne* (ed. A. Garrants).

30 VOLLARD, A. (1925), *Renoir, An Intimate Portrait*, trans. R. T. Weaver, Allen & Unwin, London, p. 115.

31 KENDALL, Richard (1988), 'Degas and the contingency of vision', *Burlington Magazine*, in press.

32 VOLLARD, A. (1928), *Degas, An Intimate Portrait*, Allen & Unwin, London.

33 RAVIN, J. G. (1981), 'The Fine Arts and Ophthalmology', *Proc. Amer. Acad. Ophthal. Course*, 171.

34 PLESCH, John (1947), *Janos, The Story of a Doctor*, Gollancz, London.

35 LEEPER, Janet (1948), *Edward Gordon Craig*, Penguin Books, Harmondsworth.

36 SIEGRIST, A. (1917), 'Gesellschaft der Schweizerischen Augenärtze', *Klin. Mbl. Augenheilk.*, 58, 601.

37 RILKE, R. M. (1917), *Rodin, The Man and his Art*, NY, 1917.

38 PATRY, A. (1917), 'Welchen Einfluss hat die Refraktion auf das Werk des Malers', *Klin. Mbl. Augenheilk.*, 58, 597.

39 Ibid.

40 LINKS, J. G. (1982), *Canaletto*, Phaidon, Oxford.

41 WILSON, A. (1958), 'A new theory of Perspective' (unpublished monograph).

42 CANTAMESSA, G. (1938), 'Occhio E Pittura', *Boll. Oculist.*, 17, 1035.

43 FRIEDLAENDER, W. (1914), *Nicolas Poussin, Die Entwicklung seiner Kunst* – Munich.

44 VASARI, G. (1550), *Lives of the Artists*, Trans. G. Bull, Penguin Books, Harmondsworth (1965), p. 197.

45 AMES, A., PROCTOR, C. A. and AMES, B. (1923), 'Vision and the Technique of Art', *Proc. Amer. Acad. Arts and Sciences*, 58, 1.

46 LIEBREICH, R. (1872), 'Turner and Mulready – On the Effect of Certain Faults of Vision on Painting, with Especial Reference to their Works', *No. Proc. Roy. Inst.*, 6, 450.

47 HUBER, O. (1932), 'Zu Grecos Astigmatismus', *Klin. Mbl. Augenheilk.*, 89, 97.
   HUBER, O. (1935), 'Aug meines publikation "Zu Grecos Astigmatismus"', *Z. Augenheilk.*, 86, 37.
   ISAKOWITZ, J. (1918), 'Zur Frage der Beziehungen Swischen Refraktion und dem Werk des Malers', *Klin. Mbl. Augenheilk.*, 61, 454.
   ISAKOWITZ, J. (1933), 'Zu Grecos Astigmatismus – (Eine Replik)', *Klin. Mbl. Augenheilk.*, 91, 110.
   MARQUEZ, M. (1926), 'Sobre el Supuerto Astigmatismo del Greco', *Arch. Oftal. Hisp.-Amer.*, 26, 715.
   MARQUEZ, M. (1929), 'El mundo exterior, la imagen retiniana y del Greco', *Rev. Espan. de Med. y Cir.*, 12, 264.
   PATRY, A. (1917), op. cit.

48 AHLSTRÖM, O. (1955), 'The Eyesight of Some Renaissance Artists', *Opt. Sci. Instr. Mkr.*, 130, 253.

49 BOZZOLI, S. (1957), *Otium (L'Occhio del mio Amico Poeta)*, Treviso.

50 WIRTH, A. (1968), 'Patologia oculare e arti figurativi', *Atti della Fondazione*.

51 HUBER, O. (1932, 1935).

52 HUGHES, R. (1974), 'An Obsession with Seeing', *Time* magazine, 8 April 1974, p. 46.

53 HARDY, W. E. (1934), *Random Reflections on Ophthalmo-Optical History, Techniques, Philosophy, Literature and Personalities*, Hatton Press, London.

Chapter 2

1 YAGER, D. and JAMESON, D. (1968), 'On Criteria for assessing type of colour vision in animals', *Anim. Behav.*, 16, p. 29.

2 VALOIS, R. de and JACOBS, G. H. (1968), 'Primate Colour Vision', *Science*, 162, p. 533.

3 MARSHALL, A. J. (1954), *Bower Birds*, Oxford University Press.

4 MORRIS, D. (1960), *The Biology of Art*, Methuen, London, p. 22.

5 HERBERT, M. and SLUKIN, W. (1969), 'Acquisition of colour preferences by chicks at different temperatures', *Anim. Behav.*, 17, p. 213.
FOSTER, John (1953), 'Curiosa Ophthalmica', *Trans. Ophthal. Soc. Australia*, 12, p. 28.

6 GLADSTONE, W. E. (1858), *Homer and the Homeric Age*, London.

7 MUELLER, Max (1887), *The Science of Thought*, Scribner, New York, p. 299.

8 HEATON, J. M. (1968), *The Eye, Phenomenology and Psychology of Function and Disorder*, Tavistock, Lippincott, London.

9 DORN, E. (1903), 'uber die Sichtbarkeit der Röntgenstrahlen für vollständig Farbenblinde', *Wiedem. Ann. Phys. Chem.*, 68, p. 1171.

10 DONNET, L. (1963), 'Couleurs et Tempraments', *Presse Méd.*, 71, p. 2008.

11 SCHAIE, K. W. (1966), 'On the Relation of Colour and Personality', *J. Project. Techn.*, 30, p. 512.

12 SPROULE, B. M. (1968), 'Colour-shift in memory for colours', Proc. 2nd Scottish Symposium on Colour, Edinburgh.

13 LANG, S. (1968), 'Colour preferences in choosing towels', Proc. 2nd Scottish Symposium on Colour, Edinburgh.

14 CERBUS, G. and NICHOLS, R. C. (1963), 'Personality Variables and Response to Colour', *Psychol. Bull.*, 60, p. 566.

15 RICKERS-OVSIANKINA, M. A., KNAPP, R. H. and McINTYRE, D. W. (1963), 'Factors affecting the psychodiagnostic significance of colour perception', *J. Project. Techn.*, 27, p. 461.

16 LEE, T.C. (1981), 'Van Gogh's Vision, Digitalis Intoxication?', *J. Amer. Med. Ass.*, 245, p.727–9.

17 CARSTAIRS, Morris (1966), 'The Madness of Art', *Observer* (Col. Supp.), 12 October 1966.

18 LAKOWSKI, R. and MONTGOMERY, G.W.G. (1968), 'Colour discrimination in profoundly deaf children', Proc. 2nd Scottish Symposium on Colour, Edinburgh.

19 CAWTHORNE, Terence (1962), 'Goya's illness', *Proc. Roy. Soc. Med.*, 55, p.213.

20 CAWTHORNE, Terence (1960), 'The influence of deafness on the creative instinct', *Laryngoscope*, 70, 1110.

21 SLATER, E. (1963), 'The Colour Imagery of Poets', *Schweizer Arch. Neurol. Psychiat.*, 91, p.303.

22 OSTWALD, P.F. (1964), 'Colour hearing: A missing link between normal perception and the hallucination', *Arch. Gen. Psychiat. (Chicago)*, 11, p.40.

23 LURIA, A.R. (1938), *The Mind of a Mnemonist*, Jonathan Cape, London.

24 MILES, W.E. (1954), 'How Colours affect us', *Today's Health*, No. 24, quoted by Schlaeger, T.F. (1957), *Psychosometric Ophthalmology*, Williams and Williams Co., Baltimore.

25 HEATON, op. cit.

26 INMAN, W.S. (1946), 'Styes, Barley and Wedding Rings', *Brit. J. Med. Psychol.*, 70, p.331.

27 DOESSCHATE, G. Ten (1946), 'Some historical notes on Spectacles and on Beryllus', *Brit. J. Ophthal.*, 30, p.660.

28 EBERS PAPYRUS, THE (*c.*1500 BC), trans. Ebbell, Levin and Munksgaard (1937), Copenhagen, p.73.

29 LUCRETIUS (*c.*60 BC), *De Rerum Natura*, Book 4, trans. Bailey (1921), Oxford, p.325.

30 BEDE, The Venerable (*c.* AD 720), 'De Natura Rerum', in *The Complete Works of the Venerable Bede*, ed. J. Giles (1843–4), London, 6, p.157.

31 YAZMAJIAN, R.V. (1968), 'Dreams completely in colour', *J. Amer. Psychol. Ass.*, 16, p.32.

32 SNYDER, F. (1965), 'Progress in the new biology of dreaming', *Amer. J. Psychiat.*, 122, p.370.
DEVEREUX, G. (1967), 'Observation and belief in Aeschylus' account of dreams', *Psychother. Psychosom.*, 17, p.114.

33 FOULKES, D., PIVIK, T., STEADMAN, H.S., SPEAR, P.S., and SYMONDS, J.D. (1967), 'Dreams of the male child', *J. Abnorm. Psychol.*, 72, p.457.

34 KARACAN, I., GOODENOUGH, R.R., SHAPIRO, A. and

STARKER, S. (1966), 'Erection cycle during sleep in relation to dream anxiety', *Arch. Gen. Psychiat. (Chicago)*, 15, p. 183.

SUINN, R. M. (1967), 'Anxiety and Colour Dreaming', *Ment. Hyg.*, 51, p. 27.

GOODENOUGH, R. R., LEWIS, H. B., SHAPIRO, A., JARET, L. and SLESER, I. (1965), 'Dream reporting', *J. Personality Soc. Psychol.*, 2, p. 170.

35 FITZGERALD, Roy G. (1971), 'Visual phenomenology in recently blind adults', *Amer. J. Psychiat.*, 127, p. 11.

36 CRICK, F. and MITCHISON, G. (1983), 'The Function of Dream Sleep', *Nature*, 304, p. 111.

ANTROBUS, J. S., DEMENT, W. and FISHER, C. (1964), 'Eye movements accompanying day dreaming, visual imagery and thought suppression', *J. Abnorm. Soc. Psychol.*, 69, 244.

37 GARMA, A. (1961), 'Colour in Dreams', *Int. J. Psychoanal.*, 42, p. 556.

38 BLUM, H. (1964), 'Colour in Dreams', *Int. J. Psychoanal.*, 45, p. 519.

39 MILLER, S. (1964), 'The manifest dream and the appearance of colour in Dreams', *Int. J. Psychoanal.*, 45, p. 512.

40 COLQUHOUN, N. C. and PALMER, H. (1953), 'Pictorial art, viewed from the standpoint of mental organisation as revealed by the excitatory abreactive techniques of psychiatry', *J. Mental Sci.*, 99, p. 136.

Chapter 3

1 MANN, Ida (1966), *Culture, Race, Climate and Eye Disease*, Thomas, Springfield, Ill.

2 POST, R. H. (1962), 'Population differences in Red and Green Colour Vision deficiency', *Eugenics Quarterly*, 9, No. 1, p. 181.

3 GALTON, Francis (1883), *Inquiries into Human Faculty*, Macmillan, London, p. 47.

4 VERNON, P. E. and STRAKER, A. (1943), 'Distribution of Colour-Blind Men in Great Britain', *Nature*, 152, p. 690.

5 PICKFORD, R. W. and COBB, S. R. (1974), 'Personality and Colour vision deficiencies', in *Modern Problems of Ophthalmology*, Eds, Streiff and Veriest, Karger, Basel, 13, pp. 225–230.

TAYLOR, G. H. (1912), 'The Colour Sense in relation to the emotions', *Lancet*, 1, p. 683.

6 BELL, J. (1926), *Treasury of Human Intelligence*, Vol. II, Cambridge.

7 RIDDELL, W. J. B. (1949), 'Discussion on Colour vision in Industry', *Proc. Roy. Soc. Med.*, 42, 145.

8 PEARSON, K. (1924), *The Life of Francis Galton*, Vol. II, Cambridge.

9 GOETHE, J. W. (1810), *Die Farbenlehre*, Cotta Verlag, Leipzig.

10 LIEBREICH, R. (1872), 'Turner and Mulready – On the Effect of certain Faults of Vision on Painting, with especial reference to their Works', *Not. Proc. Roy. Inst.*, 6, p. 450.

11 ANGELUCCI, A. (1893), *L'Occhio e la Pittura*, Lazzeri, Siena.
ANGELUCCI, A. (1908), 'Les Peintures des Daltoniens', *Rec. d Ophtal. (Paris)*, 30, p. 1.

12 ALBERTOTTI, G. (1889), *Osservazioni supra Dipinti*, Moneti, Modena.

13 BROSCHMANN, D. (1966), 'Der Farbenuntuechtige und seine Umwelt', *Klin. Mbl. Augenheilk.*, 148, 2, p. 290.

14 MAJEWSKI, K. A. (1936), 'Sur la myopie de Jean Matejko, Peintre Polonais', *Ann. Oculist. (Paris)*, 173, p. 554.

15 LAW, B. M. (1957), 'Constable and Colour', Paper read during Cdn. Ophthal. Cong. at Banff, Alberta.

16 LANTHONY, P. (1982), 'Daltonisme et Peintre', *J. Fr. Ophtalmol.*, Masson, S. A., Paris, 5, pp. 373–85.

17 PICKFORD, R. W. (1964), 'A Deuteranomalous artist', *Brit. J. Psychol.*, 55, p. 469.

18 PICKFORD, R. W. (1965), 'Two Artists with Protean Colour Vision Defects', *Brit. J. Psychol.*, 56, p. 421.

19 PICKFORD, R. W. (1967), 'Colour-defective students in Colleges of Art', *Brit. J. Aesth.*, 7, p. 132.

20 SINGER, C. (1928), *From Magic to Science*, Benn, London, p. 232.

21 WOODRUFF, A. W. (1980), 'J. M. W. Turner and some of his predecessors and successors, from the medical history', *J. Roy. Soc. Med.*, 73, p. 381.

22 LIEBREICH, op. cit.

23 GUAITA, L. (1893), *La Scienza dei Colori e la Pittura*, Lazzeri, Siena.

24 CROFT-MURRAY, E. (1959), *Decorative Painting in England, 1537–1837*, Country Life, London.

25 RAVIN, J. G. (1985), 'Monet's Cataracts', *J. Amer. Med. Ass.*, 254, pp. 394–9.

26 TAYLOR, J. R. (1983), Review in *The Times*, 29 June 1983, p. 7.

27 GUITRY, Sacha, quoted by ACTON, H. (1970), *More Memoirs of an Aesthete*, Methuen, London, p. 255.

28 ARDIZZONE, E. (1963), Personal communication.

29 ANONYMOUS (1958), Obituary of G. Rouault, *Time* magazine, 24 February 1958.

30 WALLACE, William (1888), 'The Field of Vision', MD Thesis, University of Glasgow.

31 LUCRETIUS (c.60 BC), *De Rerum Natura*, Book 4, trans. Bailey (1921), Oxford, p. 325.

32 PALMER, R. D. (1966), 'Visual Acuity and Excitement', *Psychosom. Med.*, 28, p. 364.

33 RIDLEY, F. (1952), 'Some reflections on visual perception', *Trans. Ophthal. Soc. UK*, 72, p. 635.

34 SACKS, O. and WASSERMAN, R. (1897), 'The Painter who became colour-blind', *New York Review of Books*, 34, 18.

35 CANTAMESSA, G. (1938), 'Occhio e pittura', *Boll. Oculist.*, 17, 1035.

36 PICKFORD, R. W. and TAYLOR, W. O. G. (1968), 'Colour vision of two albinos', *Brit. J. Ophthal.*, 52, No. 8, p. 640.

37 AMES, A., PROCTOR, C. A. and AMES, B. (1923), 'Vision and the technique of art', *Proc. Amer. Acad. Arts and Sciences*, 58, p. 1.

Chapter 4
===

1 FOSTER, John (1953), 'Curiosa Ophthalmica', *Trans. Ophthal. Soc. Australia*, 12, p. 28.

2 BLODI, F. (1978), 'Was Mozart Cross-eyed?', *Arch. Ophthal.*, 99, p. 822.

3 FOSS, E. (1876), *A Biographical Dictionary of the Judges of England*, Murray, London, p. 752.

4 GALVAO, P. G. (1964), 'Hypertelorism and Divergent Strabismus in the work of Aleijadinho', *Rev. Brasil. Oftal.*, 23, p. 265.

5 TORILLHON, I. M. (1958), MD Thesis, quoted in *Time* magazine, 17 February 1958.

6 BEATTIE, P. H. (1953), 'The ocular troubles of Dr Johnson and Mr Pepys', *Proc. Roy. Soc. Med.*, 6, p. 591.

7 JAMES, R. R. (1933), *Studies in the History of Ophthalmology in England Prior to 1800*, Cambridge University Press.

8 ROFE, P. C. and ANDERSON, R. S. (1970), 'Food preference in domestic pets', *Proc. Nat. Soc.*, 29, p. 330.

9 WINNICOTT, Donald W. (1944), 'Ocular Psychoneuroses', *Trans. Ophthal. Soc. UK*, 64, p. 46.

10 DALE, Rodney (1968), *Louis Wain*, Kimber, London.

11 ANONYMOUS (1981), 'Left Hand, Right Hand', Leader in *Brit. Med. J.*, 282, p. 588, 21 February 1981.

12 BARSLEY, M. (1966), *The Left-Handed Book*, Souvenir Press, London.

13 HERMELIN, B. and O'CONNOR, N. (1971), *Nature*, June 18, p. 470 (corres.).

14 BRYDEN, M. P. (1966), 'Left-right differences in Tachistoscopic recognitions', *Percept. Motor Skills*, 23, p. 1127.

15 OLTMAN, P. K. and CAPOBIANCO, R. (1967), 'Field dependence and Eye Dominance', *Percept. Motor Skills*, 25, p. 645.

16 GAFFRON, M. (1950), 'Right and left in pictures', *Art Quarterly*, 13, p. 312.
GAFFRON, M. (1962), 'Phenomenal properties and perceptual organizations', in '*Psychology: A Study of a Science*', Vol. 4, 'Biologically orientated fields', ed. Koch, McGraw Hill, NY, p. 562.

17 HOVSEPIAN, W., SLAYMAKER, F. and JOHNSON, J. (1980), 'Handedness as determinant of L-R placement in human figure-drawings', *J. Personality Assessment*, 44, pp. 470–3.

18 SWARTZ, R. and HEWITT, D. (1970), 'Lateral organization in HUBER, O. (1935), 'Vergleichende Augenheilkunde', *Klin. Mbl. Augenheilk.*, 95, p. 574.

19 WEINSTEIN, P. (1958), *Szemünk Vilaga*, Budapest.

20 ROSS, B. M. (1966), 'Minimal Familiarity and Left-Right Judgement of Paintings', *Percept. Motor Skills*, 22, p. 105.

21 GARDNER, Martin (1967), *The Ambidextrous Universe*, Allen Lane, London.

22 ARRUGA, A. (1984), 'Sidedness, writing and art. Significance in some problems related to oculomotricity', *Doc. Ophthal.*, 58, p. 11–23.
POPHAM, A. E. (1946), *The Drawings of Leonardo da Vinci*, Jonathan Cape, London.

23 LINKSZ, A. (1965), 'An ophthalmologist looks at art and artists', *Proc. Amer.-Hungarian Med. Ass.*, 1, p. 1.

24 DREWRY, Yvonne (1968), Report in *East Anglian Times*, 8 May 1968.

Chapter 5

1 SCARLETT, E. P. (1964), 'A Doctor comments on Bach', *Arch. Intern. Med. (Chicago)*, 113, p. 449.

2 LARSSON, S. (1965), *Konstnärens Öga*, Stockholm.

3 NORTHCOTE, J. (1818), *Life of Sir Joshua Reynolds*, 2nd ed., Henry Colburn, London, p. 246.

4 CHANCE, Burton (1939), 'Sir Joshua Reynolds and his blindness and death', *Ann. Med. Hist.*, 3, p. 487.

CHAMBERS, W. and R. (eds) (1863), *The Book of Days*, London and Edinburgh, p. 289.

5 WATERHOUSE, E. K. (1941), *Reynolds*, Kegan Paul, Trench Trubner & Co., London.

6 JAMES, W. (1967), Editorial in *Insight*, November–December 1967, p. 3.

7 FRANCESCHETTI, A. (1939), 'Sur le rapport entre phosphènes mécaniques provoqués et certaines affections oculaires', Congr. Soc. Franc. O.N.O. Bordeaux, 3 June 1938, *Cite Rev. O.N.O.*, 17, p. 244.
LEBER, T. (1877), 'Die Angeborene Amaurose durch Retinal-atrophie', *Graefe-Saemisch Handb. Augenheilk.*, I, 5, p. 648.

8 KELLOG, Rhoda, KNOLL, M. and KUGLER, J. (1965), 'Form-similarity between Phosphenes of Adults and pre-school Children's scribblings', *Nature*, 208, p. 1129.

9 SPERDUTO, R. (1983), 'Senile macular dystrophy, an artist's view', *J. Amer. Med. Ass.*, 250, p. 2507.

10 THURBER, J. (1968), *My Life and Hard Times*, Harper and Row, New York, pp. 7–8.

11 BROWN, E. G. (1934), *Milton's Blindness*, Columbia University Press, New York.

12 WILMER, W. H. (1933), 'The Blindness of Milton', *Bull. Int. Hist. Med.*, 1, p. 85.

13 ROGERS, L. (1949), 'John Milton's Blindness: a suggested diagnosis', *J. Hist. Med.*, 4, p. 468.

14 LEWIS, Wyndham (1951), *Listener*, 10 May 1951.

15 SAVIN, L. (1958), 'Influence of vascular changes in progressive failure of vision', *Trans. Ophthal. Soc. UK*, 78, p. 315.

16 MOONEY, A. J. et al. (1965), 'Parasagittal parieto-occipital men-ingioma with visual hallucinations', *Amer. J. Ophthal.*, 59, pp. 197–205.

17 DONGEN, H. R. and VAN FORTUYN, J. D. (1968), 'Drawing with closed eyes', *Psychiat. Neurol. Neurochir.*, 71, p. 275.

18 SINGER, C. (1928), *From Magic to Science*, Benn, London, p. 232.

19 HENBLEST, N. (1982), 'A long year's journey into night', *New Scientist*, 25 February 1982, p. 131.

20 HUXLEY, Aldous (1954), *The Doors of Perception*, Penguin Books, Harmondsworth, p. 19.

21 ELLIS, Havelock (1898), quoted by R. Gainsborough in *Medical News*, 21 February 1898, p. 13.

22 DALE, Rodney (1968), *Louis Wain*, Kimber, London.

23 SCHNECK, J. M. (1965), 'Macropsie', *Amer. J. Psychiat.*, 121, p. 1123.

24 SCHOPLER, E. (1966), 'Birth order and preference between visual and tactile receptors', *Percept. Motor Skills*, 22, p. 74.

25 LOWENFELD, V. (1939), *The Nature of Creative Artistry*, Routledge and Kegan Paul, London.
   LOWENFELD, Victor (1951), 'Psychoaesthetic Implications of the Art of the Blind', *J. Aesthetics and Art Criticism*, 10, p. 1.

Chapter 6

1 GIFFORD, Edward S. (1958), *The Evil Eye*, Macmillan, New York.
2 KEELE, K. D. (1955), 'Leonardo da Vinci on Vision', *Proc. Roy. Soc. Med.*, 48, p. 384.
3 RUSS, Charles (1921), 'An Instrument set in motion by vision or by the proximity of the human body', *Lancet*, ii, p. 222.
4 HEATON, J. M. (1968), *The Eye, Phenomenology and Psychology of Function and Disorder*, Tavistock, Lippincott, London.
5 INMAN, W. S. (1965), 'Emotional Factors in Corneal Disease', *Brit. J. Med. Psychol.*, 38, p. 277.
6 COHN, Hermann (1882), 'Eye Disease and Masturbation', *Arch. Ophthal.*, 1, p. 428.
7 POWER, H. (1887), 'Relation of ophthalmic disease to certain normal and pathological conditions of the sexual organs', *Trans. Ophthal. Soc. UK*, 7, p. 1.
8 AGARWAL, K. M. (1964), 'The cause of defective eyesight and fundamental principles of normal sight', *Med. Digest (Bombay)*, 32, 471.
9 GIFFORD, op. cit.
10 FOSTER, J. (1953), 'Curiosa Ophthalmica', *Trans. Ophthal. Soc. Australia*, 12, p. 28.
11 VILLEY, Pierre (1930), *The World of the Blind*, trans. Alys Hallard, Duckworth, London.
12 DOBRONRAVOV, S. N. and FISHELEV, Y. R., 'Cutaneous Vision', *Fed. Proc. Transl. Suppl.*, 29, p. 659.
13 FRENCH, C. N. (1965), 'Tactile Vision, Thermal and Texture cues in the discrimination of black and white', *Nature (London)*, 208, p. 1352.
14 MAKOUS, W. L. (1966), 'Cutaneous Colour Sensitivity', *Psychol. Review*, 73, p. 292.
   SNYAKIN, P. G. (1965), 'Relationship between optics and cutaneous perception of Light in man', *Fed. Proc. Transl. Suppl.*, 24, p. 661.
   STEINBERG, D. D. (1966), 'Light sensed through Receptors in the Skin'. *Amer. J. Psychol.*, 79, p. 324.
   STEVEN, D. M. (1963), 'The Dermal Light Sense', *Biol. Rev.*, 38, p. 204.

15 EWART, A. G. and CARP, F. M. (1963), 'Recognition of Tactual forms by sighted and blind subjects', *Amer. J. Psychol.*, 76, p. 488.

16 FRY, Sara Margery (1954), *Old Age Looks at Itself*, National Old People's Welfare Council, London, p. 4, reprinted from 'Old Age in the Modern World', report of the third Congress of Int. Assoc. of Gerontology, London, 1954.

17 WILSON, Sir J. F. (1948), 'Adjustments to Blindness', *Brit. J. Psychol.*, 38, p. 218.

18 COATES, W. H. (1939), *Beating Shoes*, Heath Cranston Ltd, London.

19 SCHUMANN, H.-J. von (1955), 'Phanomenologische und Psychoanalytische untersuchung des Homerische Traume', *Acta Psychother. (Basel)*, 3, p. 205.

20 BORGES, Jorge Luis (1968), An account of his blindness, in an interview at Harvard, January 1968.

21 SCARLETT, E. P. (1964), 'A Doctor comments on Bach', *Arch. Intern. Med. (Chicago)*, 113, p. 449.

22 JAMES, R. R. (1933), *Studies in the History of Ophthalmology in England prior to 1800*, Cambridge University Press, p. 90.

23 JACKSON, D. M. (1968), 'Bach, Handel and the Chevalier Taylor', *Med. Hist.*, 12, p. 385.

24 LOWENFELD, V. (1951), 'Psychoaesthetic implications of the art of the blind', *J. Aesthetics and Art-criticism*, 10, p. 1.

25 RÉVÉSZ, G. (1950), *Psychology and Art of the Blind*, trans. H. Wolff, Longmans Green, London.

26 LOCKE, John (1690), *Essay Concerning Human Understanding*, Locke's *Essays*, II, 9, 8.

27 BERKELEY, George, Bishop of Cloyne (1709), *Essay Towards a New Theory of Vision*, printed by Aaron Rhames for Jeremy Pepyat, Dublin.

28 ROCK, I. and HARRIS, C. S. (1967), 'Vision and Touch', *Sci. American*, 216, p. 96.

29 CHESELDEN, William (1728), 'An account of Observations made by a young gentleman ...', *Philosoph. Trans. (April–June)*, 7–402, p. 447.

30 WARE, James (1810), 'Case of a young gentleman who recovered his sight when seven years of age after having been deprived of it by cataracts before he was a year old; with remarks', *Philosoph. Trans.*, 91, p. 382.

31 WARDROP, James (1826), 'Case of a lady born blind, who received sight at an advanced age by the formation of an artificial pupil', *Philos. Trans.*, 116, p. 529.

32 FISHER, C. M. (1964), 'The later acquisition of vision by Persons born Blind', *Trans. Amer. Neurol. Ass.*, 89, p. 195.

33 SENDEN, M. von (1932), *Space and Sight*, trans. Peter Heath (1960), Butler and Tanner Ltd, Frome and London.

34 GREGORY, R. L. and WALLACE, J. G. (1963), *Recovery from Early Blindness*, E.P.S. Monograph, No. 2, Cambridge.

Appendix

==

1 PALMER, R. D. (1966), 'Visual acuity and excitement', *Psychosom. Med.*, 28, p. 364.

2 STEVENS, D. and WOLFF, H. (1905), 'The Relationship of Myopia to performance on a test of levelling-sharpening', *Percept. Motor Skills*, 21, 399.

3 YOUNG, F. A. (1967), 'Myopia and personality', *Amer. J. Optom.*, 44, p. 192.

4 BECKER, G. (1965), 'Visual Acuity, Birth order, Achievement versus Affiliation, and Other Edwards Personal Preference Schedule Scores', *J. Psychom. Res.*, 9, 277.

5 OSBORNE, H. (1968), 'Colour Concepts of the Ancient Greeks', *Brit. J. Aesthetics*, 8, 269.

6 DOUGLAS, W. O. (1950), *Strange Lands and Friendly People*, Harper, New York.

INDEX